for My Mother,
Margaret Mary Shaver
who showed me the way

for my nieces,
Erin, Kelsey, and Madison,
my great-niece, Parker,
my godchild, Brooke,
my adopted nieces,
Marissa, Alexandra, Julia,
Sabrina, and Jackie

No ray of sunlight is ever lost,
but the green which it wakes into
existence needs time to sprout,
and it is not always granted the power
to live to see the harvest.
All work that is worth anything is done in faith.
—Albert Schweitzer—

Contents

Preface

WOMEN ARE THE keepers of the flame. They are the hearth of the home and of relationship. Women are mothers, bearers of life and nurturer of others. Yet what happens when the keepers of the hearth grow tired and no longer tend to their own fires?

What happens when the role of nurturer becomes confused or overly enmeshed with the place of belonging of the inner woman? Something goes terribly wrong. The fire goes out and the hearth grows cold.

For the last thirty-five years, I have been a psychotherapist in private practice and I've also led workshops for women. For as long as I can remember, women have been motivated to discuss and improve their relationships. Lately, however, I am observing a different trend, an emotional shift of sorts. I hear women longing to check out emotionally, as opposed to expressing a desire to check in. After spending hundreds of hours sitting at the hearths of women and listening to their stories, and I include my own story in the picture, I believe women have come to the end of their collective rope.

Intellectually, women have gone the distance when it comes to sorting out how to "do it all" while simultaneously caring for others as well as themselves. From my professional vantage point, which is experientially based as opposed to research based, women are quietly rebelling while paradoxically still trying to fit it all in. Aware or not, women seem to be collectively refusing to fit into a paradigm that no longer suits their authentic feminine nature.

Fortunately, there is a way to live beyond the deadening experience of unconsciously defaulting to the role of emotional caretaker of others, or working on "it." New meaning and promise

Find out who you are and do it on purpose.

—

Dolly Parton

can be found in the presence of the mysterious feminine, the keeper of the flames of love and life. All that is required to walk the path that leads you out of your head into the garden of your heart is to gently welcome and give in to the *mystical call of knowing* that emanates from within and beckons you forth, inward.

Of course, with these last words comes the tricky part. How does a modern-day woman find the time to let go and give in to the soothing aspect of her nature without thinking she will lose her mind, and fail in her responsibilities to care for those she loves, which for many women signals the loss of what she prizes most, a loving relationship? Mostly, how do you accomplish the task of opening up your heart without adding one more thing to your "to do" list, the heavy load you already carry? Let's take a look.

Recently, a woman came to my office and shared that secretly she hadn't wanted to keep her appointment. She was tired of "working on…it"—mainly, herself. She was exhausted from all of her effort to better herself. Encouraged by her willingness to be truthful with what was going on inside her, I asked if she would like to try something different. I asked if she would allow me to take over/do the "work part" of the session so she could sit back and mindfully observe within herself what it felt like to actively reconnect with the woman within while receiving support.

Immediately she lit up. "You mean I don't have to work on anything?"

"That's right," I said. "Sometimes it's about trusting that you have done your part and that it is time to pause, open your heart, and just receive." With a huge sigh, she sat back in the couch and began the next cycle of her becoming.

As my client left the session, she commented on how much better, lighter, she felt. "Funny, it's not that we didn't 'do' anything," she said. "We did. It's just that the way we mentally approached the task was different. I liked that we framed the session as an invitation so that I could freely *reconnect* with myself, as opposed to thinking about having to *work* on myself." She paused, before adding, "What is interesting to me is that by allowing you to hold a space for my opening up, I went so much deeper. I recovered parts of me…." Eyes sparkling, she left the session telling me she was going to practice giving herself breathing room. She would imagine me holding a space so that she could freely let go and venture inward.

To empower the mysterious feminine, sometimes all you need is someone to hold the space of your unfolding, the way a trainer spots for a gymnast. Then, with support, you are able to let go of control and gently delve into yourself knowing you are safe. From a nurturing paradigm, you can begin the journey of differentiating who you are as a woman separate from the unconscious default role of emotional caretaker of others—a blind spot that keeps you looping around in circles and out of relationship with yourself. With someone to spot what you cannot see, you can reverse the role reversal, set yourself free, and thus expand your capacity to give and receive love, which is the ultimate intent, the singular journey laid out for you in *Lipstick and Soul.*

The Invitation

THE KEY: I know that, as women, we are drawn to relationship. We love our hearths and tending to their fires. It's in our nature. So, before you turn away from your heart because you do not have a map to lead you inward, let me extend an invitation. As I did with my client, I invite you to try something different. I invite you to pause and take a moment to accept the offer to go within. In doing so, I invite you to free your mind, put your feet up, and let me do the heavy lifting.

Armchair Travel

WHEN I TRAVEL, I like to know a little about the journey ahead. For example, what is the weather going to be like? What activities will I be engaging in? With that in mind, what clothes do I bring? Will I take side trips and, if so, to see what? How will I get along with the person or people I'm traveling with? How will we negotiate the need for separate activities, time/space, and moods? I'm assuming you are similar. So, for your convenience, in this section of *Lipstick and Soul,* I have laid out some details about the journey ahead.

The Title: *Lipstick and Soul*

I CHOSE THE title *Lipstick and Soul* to convey a message of lightheartedness with depth. I know this sounds contradictory. Yet I believe the paradoxical concept is representative of the mysterious feminine, which is a state of being that is simultaneously elusive, while being very present, a little like the light and magnetic power of the moon.

I also like the title because my inner woman perks up whenever she discovers new ways to look pretty and feel restored. Judging by the numerous beauty magazines purchased every month, I know I'm not alone. Many of you must share these same thoughts and motivations.

As a way to use the imagination to get around the intellect, I decided to create a bridge through the title *Lipstick and Soul* to bring you directly into the heart of the feminine experience.

There is another reality. Because of my work, I have the opportunity to see firsthand how beautiful a woman becomes when she lets down, moves beyond her defenses, and, transformed, opens her heart to love and emotional vulnerability. Full of inner resources, she is more present and capable of being in relationship. So why not bring the idea of emotional vulnerability out of the Dark Ages? Instead of looking at it through a lens of weakness, let's reconsider the tender state as a wonderful inner resource, nature's beauty balm, an emotional moisturizer that, when properly utilized in small doses, restores facial glow, sparkle to the eyes, and stature that projects self-worth and confidence.

The Journey

WE ARE ALL the same and we are all different. To honor this truth, the format of the book is designed to fit your needs. To discover your pace and to familiarize yourself with the terrain ahead, I invite you to begin your journey by reading the book cover to cover. You may want to compare the moment to stepping up to a perfume counter and testing different perfumes before deciding, with assistance, which fragrance suits you best. In the same way that your selection of perfume is the result of spending time at the perfume counter, your journey of self-discovery is cumulative. As you move through each chapter, you will find yourself quietly led deeper within, leaving behind your blind spots, the defense mechanisms that no longer work for you. Ultimately, you are provided with an integrative mind-body-heart experience that has the intent to bring you back into loving relationship with the mysterious feminine, the strong presence and holder of your place of emotional belonging.

The Book

I THINK OF the journey in *Lipstick and Soul* as a trilogy divided into three distinct and different parts. They include: Be Bold (Book One); Be Beautiful (Book Two); and Be True to Yourself (Book Three). The three parts, when put together, mirror a comprehensive journey of emotional renewal and integration.

Book One: BE BOLD

IN THIS BOOK you accept the invitation to try something different, to be fresh and more open. In doing so, you turn toward a new way of being and saying "Yes" to becoming…

In the initial stages of the journey, which take place in chapters one through four, you have the chance to evaluate how open you are. Through a self-assessment questionnaire, you will pinpoint the specific areas that hold you back, the ones that keep you stuck, "working it," and out of tune with yourself. To create a refreshed focal point for your travels, you will be given the opportunity to become present with yourself by airing out some of your current upsets—guilt-free, of course.

The main intent embedded in Book One is to prepare you to leave the old (defenses) behind and open up to the new (your best authentic self). Keeping the theme of beauty in mind, let's create a comparative perspective for this part of the journey: Think of this section as a necessary beauty scrub to unclog pores and bring new skin to the surface.

Book Two: BE BEAUTIFUL

THIS BOOK, DIVIDED into two phases, brings you to a moment of truth. When *sans* makeup, you naturally open up. You learn to see, experience, and accept yourself. In this state of openness, I believe you are most beautiful and powerful because you are in your element. You are in the essence of your authentic feminine presence.

Learning to experience your experiences is the theme of this part of your journey. In chapters five through eight, with support, you will continue to discern and identify your hidden blocks, the unconscious barriers/mindsets that keep you out of the garden of your heart. Keeping the effort light, you are invited to participate in self-reflection experiences that help re-orient you toward hearing/reconnecting with the song of your heart.

In phase two, chapters nine through thirteen, after gaining strength you begin to make headway through the gauntlet, the inner path which leads you out of your head and into your heart.

Along the way, you will encounter the guards (the talking heads) who make it difficult for you to keep your course. You know the ones, the emotional saboteurs who falsely misguide you into believing they are protecting you when, in fact, they are undermining you. They are the ones who tell you that emotional vulnerability is a weakness, a disease you don't want to catch.

For clarity, let's continue with the beauty metaphor: Think of the guards (your defense mechanism, the part that is always "working it") as the voice of temptation that seductively tells you that you deserve to eat one more piece of luscious chocolate and, furthermore, that it will not show up on your face or your thighs. Right!

Book Three: BE TRUE TO YOURSELF

In the final stages of your journey that take place in chapters fourteen through sixteen, you enter into the sanctuary of the mysterious, where all is possible. Once inside, you are able to access the voices of your authentic self, the inner woman, the wonderful and capricious Wise Woman, as well as the spirit of the mysterious. It is here, in the garden of your deepest and most sacred self—your soul—that you receive the gift of knowing you are loved. You realize from the bottom of your heart that you can only give to others what you give to yourself first.

With the experiential awareness available to you, you naturally come into balance. You discover an inner place of peace where the masculine and feminine live side by side, in the service of one another, available to help you become the unique woman you are. It is here, in this place of authentic energy that the essence of your feminine presence dwells. When you fully own your feminine presence, you are consciously present and free to become yourself while in relationship with those you love. For the sake of our mutual understanding, when I mention the word *present*, I mean that you are fully conscious, aware of, and living from your authentic, cognitive, and emotional states of being. Returning to the beauty metaphor, think of this part of your journey as discovering the perfect customized luxurious skincare products you integrate into your beauty routine.

For Overall Clarification

FOR THE SAKE of continuity, when I mention the concept of the *inner feminine and mysterious feminine*, I am referring to a wonderful, warm, loving, all-embracing, humane energy that resides within each one of us as well as all around us. When I mention *feminine presence*, I am referring to all of the above, with an added bonus. I see feminine presence as a portal for a connection with a divine presence, a universal truth beyond. That said I do not intend to influence your way of interpreting such a presence other than to ask you to entertain the thought that such a presence exists. Ultimately, I wholeheartedly invite you to integrate your idea of such a divine presence into your journey in any way you see fit. For clarification purposes, I will be describing divine presence as feminine.

Now, let's get to the practical aspects of your journey:

Chapter Format

EACH CHAPTER BEGINS with a thematic lesson to support your forward movement. It is followed by a personal story (called author's story) from my own experience. The intent of the story is to give you the sense that you are not traveling alone, and to be used as a teaching tool. As I mentioned earlier, I will do the holding. The embedded intent of the chapter content is to nourish your heart and soothe your soul. Finally, each chapter represents a necessary stepping stone that is part of an overall transformation journey.

Quotes

AT THE BEGINNING of every chapter is a quotation. You are invited to use the quote as a daily self-reflection tool. The quotes are sequentially laid out to create a progressive experience of going within. These are wonderful gems for those of you who are new to opening up emotionally. You will also notice quotes before writing exercises and also at the end of each chapter. The quotes are intended to provoke your imagination and enhance your writing exploration.

The Beauty of Writing

THE WONDERFUL SEGMENT found in each chapter signals the beginning of the interactive experience for that chapter and as such is an invitation to your unconscious to come out and play. The interactive writing experiences, called *Write Your Heart Out*, are intended to bring insight into what is going on just below the surface of your conscious awareness. Purposefully, the *Write Your Heart* Out exercises help you circumvent the intellect and provide you with direct access into your heart, the home of your felt/experiential awareness.

Please note that The Beauty of Writing sections, although similar, vary in their overall sequencing format. For example, to stimulate curiosity, thought and or creativity, you will find small segments of psych education and true stories strewn in between some of the Write Your Heart Out exercises. The intent behind the format is to create an experiential-awareness-flow much like what you find in a yoga flow class when various poses are integrated into one overall movement.

Write Your Heart Out

YOU WILL NOTICE that each Write Your Heart Out exercise is numbered and categorized by theme. This feature is for your convenience so that at the end of the book you will have a reference point for all of the work you have done. The feature allows you to set up an ongoing, customized writing practice, the details of which you will find in the Appendix section of this book.

A Writing Journal

SOME OF THE Write Your Heart Out experiences take you on a writing journey that is longer in length than others. I will note these *journal writing* exercises when they come up. For these writings, I recommend that you keep a writing journal close by. In your journal, please make sure to write the number of the Write Your Heart Out exercise you are engaged in. The number is found next to the Write Your Heart Out header. This special feature helps you keep track of the prompts from which your writing emanated.

Special Note: If at any time you feel in your heart of hearts that you should not engage in the writing exercises in this book, trust yourself. Don't do them. Writing is not for everyone. The good news is that you will still benefit from reading the book and honoring your voice, which, of course, is the purpose of the journey you are taking. On the other hand, I do encourage you to contemplate the purpose of the exercise.

Write Your Heart Out (cultivating resonance)

JUST AS IT says, this little feature is where you capture the essence of what you are exploring. At the end of your journey, you will gather all of your resonant recordings and use them to set up your customized self-care practice.

Lavender Notes

LAVENDER IS AN herb known for its soothing properties. The wonderful aroma is known to calm your mind and soothe your heart. There are moments in the book when I want to give you a little heads-up to support the depth of the work you are doing, as well as offer some encouragement. Hopefully, you will love reading these notes as much as I enjoyed thinking of you when I wrote them.

Beauty Metaphor

I LIKE USING metaphors to explain an important point I am trying to share. This is the part in the book where I indulge in that pleasure. Plus, I really want to keep a frame of beauty for the inner woman top of mind! Hopefully, the idea will stick and motivate you to care for the inner part of yourself as much as you care for your outer appearances.

Our Story: Imagine

I LOVE THIS little segment that I wrote with you in mind. Because I believe change takes place in the context of relationship, I decided to make up a story about us and use it as a teaching tool.

You will find Our Story segments strewn throughout the book. They will pop up every so often to remind you that you are not traveling alone. You have a fellow traveler—me!—by your side at all times. Each segment ends with a simple phrase: "To be continued…." This indicates that the journey will resume. There is more to come!

A Little Lipstick, If You Please!

YOU WILL DISCOVER this capricious section at the end of every chapter. The little segment provides you with cool homework assignments to keep the exploration you are engaged in fresh and dynamic. The suggestions are meant to support your opening-up process, as well as help you cultivate a practice of feminine presence.

Acknowledgments

THE JOURNEY RECOUNTED in this book was supported over many years by my husband and my friends, who encouraged me to keep writing, inspired my thinking, and acted as sounding boards and cushions of comfort when I needed it.

In particular, I am indebted to my husband, Robert Carmine, whose spirit of perseverance and renewal is a beacon of light that inspires me to keep going—to never give up, no matter what!

With gratitude, I give special thanks to my lifelong girl-friends Geri Baur, Christine Cuddy, Barbara Mayer, and Carole Marissael—who each listened attentively for years to my work in progress and never lost interest.

I especially want to mention my friend Dr. Carol Booth Olson, who took time out of her busy work schedule to edit the first couple of renditions of the book. As a nationally known author and educator in the field of writing and literature, her encouragement to put my voice "out there" meant the world to me.

Everyone needs to be accountable. I want to give a heartfelt thanks to Lisa Neil for her annual ornament party, during which when it came my turn to give "the year that was, report in," I had to say, "The book is still in progress." Thank you to the group of women who never forgot my endeavor and were always curious. Finally, this year, I can report in: "The book—the journey—is complete."

Thank you to Rhonda Gunner, Amy Guttman, and Miriam Muscarolas for being part of my support net over the years. I would like to give a heartfelt thank you to Cher Day Mann for the nurturing soups she provided my family during times of need and writing deadlines.

Professionally, I am indebted to Dr. Pat Ogden, founder of the Sensorimotor Psychotherapy Institute and internationally recognized authority in the field of trauma. The five years' training to receive the Sensorimotor Psychotherapy Certification were some of the most energizing and eye-opening moments in my life, both personally and professionally.

The integration of the body in the mind-body-spirit aspect of the journey detailed in this book is due to Dr. Ogden's influence. In addition, the fact that she introduced me to the work of Dr. Ron Kurtz plays a large part in the segments on character strategies. Dr. Ron Kurtz' categories of character strategies are integrated into the book and used much like scaffolding on a home under construction. I would, therefore, separately like to acknowledge Dr. Ron Kurtz' work. From personal experience, I found the types of character strategies helpful in providing a map to move beyond the blocks within. I have tweaked some of the names and ideas to suit the work my readers will be doing as they embark upon this journey with me.

A special thank you to Dotti Albertine—book designer extraordinaire. With her expertise the self-discovery/inner beauty guide I had envisioned came to fruition.

Introduction

Journey to Womanhood

ONE MOMENT IN time completes a journey of transitions. There is always a pause when all the questions you wonder about miraculously come to light and become integrated into new wisdom. Without any effort on your part, pieces of a puzzle fall into place. Like a knock on the door, the tap on your heart lets you know it is time to rest, that all is well. You intuit that you have come full circle. The work for that season in your life is over. You stop and ponder all that has gone on between the moment your journey started and the moment your journey came to fruition. You know it is time to pass on the lessons you learned, not because you want to pontificate—there was too much pain for that—but because from a place of heartfelt kinship, you want to share.

In the same way, I would like to share with you just such a moment in the journey of becoming. From a personal and professional perspective, I would like to impart to you some of the initial stepping stones I found to be of great value, especially when you cross bridges that lead you out of one paradigm of living and into another world of being.

The final step in my journey is where the journey in this book begins.

One is not born, but rather becomes, a woman.

—

Simone de Beauvoir

My Mother's Whisper *(author's story)*

"THIS IS WHERE I was happiest," was the voice that spoke to me from somewhere inside of myself. I was with my East Coast cousins and my sister Annie. We had taken the ferry from

*Sometimes a person
has to go back,
really back—to
have a sense, an
understanding
of all that's gone
to make them—
before they can go
forward.*

—

Paule Marshall

Portland, Maine, to Peaks Island. The sun was shining. The water was sparkling, blue. Trees were starting to turn. Apples were ripe enough to pick. It was warm as we all took off on our rented bikes to tour the island. We had a couple of hours before we had to turn the bikes in, have lunch, jump back on the ferry, and head home for another round of post-wedding events. All was good with the world.

We had arrived at the far side of the island, on schedule. Full of laughter, gliding down a hill with a breeze stroking my face, I intuited my mother's voice again: "This is what it was like for us, before…" The message trailed off. I knew exactly what my mother's presence was referring to. She, her mother, and four siblings had been vacationing on Peaks Island some seventy-five years earlier when the event happened—the knock on the door that one night changed my mother's life forever. "Ma'am, there's been an accident. Please come with us," was the lie that spilled off lips of the officer standing on the porch. My mother and her siblings were immediately packed into a police speedboat and rushed back to Portland. My Irish grandfather, an internal investigator for the Portland police department, had suffered a violent, suspicious death.

Prohibition was in full swing. My mother's father, who was due to testify in court the next day, never took the stand.

I never knew the circumstances surrounding my grandfather's death until I was in my twenties. My mother had too much pain and fear locked up inside her to speak openly about what had happened. Her secret was part of my emotional legacy. So there I was on Peaks Island, hearing her sweet voice mystically talking to me from somewhere beyond. As I listened, I imagined her riding her bike on the same path I was on, laughing as I was. With every corner I turned and each new vista that appeared, I realized I was mysteriously being given the felt experience and insight into my mother's authentic heart before it was so tragically wounded, broken. Instinctively, I knew my mother wanted me to see her for who she truly was and had been before the pain set in. What my mother could never talk about during her life, she was now inspiring *me to explore.*

The Emotional Glass Ceiling

As I LEFT the island, I felt different. With each wave of realization that washed over me, I felt a shift, a lightening up inside of me. I experienced a deep calm. I felt complete, like I had come full circle. When the shifting settled, I felt whole and reenergized.

As a psychotherapist who believes unexplored emotional ruptures can unconsciously be passed on from one generation to the next, I now also knew firsthand that they can be healed with time, patience, love, and understanding. Having previously discovered an emotional glass ceiling in myself, I received confirmation that you can only become the woman you are meant to be when you are first living from the truth of your authentic self. The gift my mother gave me on my journey to Peaks Island was a heartfelt knowing that my roots are based in love and laughter, not tragedy and pain.

Where My Mother's Journey Left Off

THE JOURNEY TO bridge the distance, the gap between the legacy of joy and the legacy of pain, had been mine to decide to take. My mother had her journey, as did her mother before her. To find my inner place of *emotional belonging,* I had to retrace some of my mother's footsteps. I had to face some pain caused by my mother's inability to be completely emotionally available. I had to get reacquainted with my authentic needs, put them first, and allow them to matter, which is how I came to be on Peaks Island. I was following an intuition/message from the inner Wise Woman to make sure I visited the place my mother had spent her summers.

What is interesting to me is that I did not know, when I stepped onto Peaks Island, that I would bring to fruition a cycle of personal transformation, a phase in my overall life journey. Yet the moment brought me into a new paradigm of living that was full of feminine presence and possibility. The journey associated with the paradigm shift is one I want to share with you.

Coming to a place of emotional contentment took time. During the sometimes difficult process, I came face to face with a realization: All of the knowledge I had gained over thirty-five years as a marriage and family therapist in private practice did not matter because, in the end, *you can't change without experiencing change.* Ultimately, much to my temporary dismay, I learned that, for change to really stick, I had to get out of my head and into my heart. I could not just talk about reconnecting with the woman within. I had to experience, own, and integrate the mysterious inner place of feminine belonging.

Opening Up, Forward

DURING MY INNER travels, one of the most interesting observations I experienced is that change does not take place in a linear fashion. Change is sensuous, somewhat messy. Also, change is like a hologram. Every part of change mirrors every other part of change. There is sadness, delight, anger, and irritation, as well as insights along with regressions and major leaps of faith, all mixed together in one complete experience of emotional growth.

Relationship First

FORTUNATELY, AS I walked the Path of Becoming, I discovered a silver lining. I learned that the more responsibility I took for caring for my authentic emotional needs, the more I felt I mattered and was in sync with my true self! I received a wonderful bonus when I realized that, by changing the relationship I had with myself, I discovered new ways of being in relationship with those I loved.

I grew to understand just how important it is for change to take place within the context of relationship. Paradoxically, and contrary to popular opinion, I learned a beautiful truth: The more "selfish" I was when implementing my emotional needs the more generously I acknowledged and listened to the needs of others.

Most of all, I learned how to unfold, and emotionally flow forward, instead of hoping for—forcing or talking about—the changes I wanted to come my way. The truth is, most of us have an inner story that limits us from fully opening up, emotionally. I am no different. In my earlier attempts at writing this book, I tried to speak about emotional vulnerability while safely hiding behind my professional demeanor, but I couldn't. Ultimately, keeping distant seemed to defeat my purpose, which was to share with you how to be yourself while being in relationship.

My Intent

ONE OF THE most heartfelt desires I have in sharing with you the nuances of reclaiming your heart is to demystify the process of opening up inside of yourself. I would like to help you realize that the process of going within is not a path to be feared; it is instead a journey full of unanticipated riches and personal discoveries. So that your efforts to shift into new ways of being do not take place in an emotional vacuum, I would like you to think of us as two women traveling together. For this purpose, I created segments for the journey called "Our Story."

Let's take a look at how I imagine "Our Story."

Our Story: Imagine…

WE ARE TWO women who separately signed up for a guided restorative walking trek through the hills and valleys of a beautiful countryside. At this moment, we find ourselves meandering through a lush, green meadow toward a river that lies at the edge of a field beyond. The birds are chirping. It is a warm, sunny day. A slight, tepid breeze is blowing. We are savoring the smell of fresh dirt and the fragrance of wildflowers.

Together, we marvel at the luxury of having all day to get to where we are going. We chuckled at the thought that someone other than ourselves is setting up the daily itinerary. Aside from our private reasons for taking this journey, we feel carefree.

As we walk along, you find out that I am a psychotherapist who specializes in in-depth process work. By the passion in my voice, you assess accurately that women's issues hold a special place in my heart. I find out you are a woman who cares deeply for those you love; for your own personal reasons you are taking time to get back in touch with yourself. By the vulnerable and slightly weary tone in your voice, I gather that taking time for yourself is a journey that for you is long overdue.

As we wander along, we find kinship in a discussion about how difficult it is for us to take time to nurture our hearts. We discuss how paradoxical it is that women give themselves permission to take time and spend money on outer beauty, yet feel selfish when they attend in the smallest way to their inner emotional needs. We agree wholeheartedly that, apart from an occasional spa treatment, a girls' night out here and there, and going to the gym, most women do not put themselves on their own priority list, let alone at the top of their list, unless they need to recuperate from an illness or an emotional crisis. Together, we chuckle at the mutual recognition of the rare occasions when we opened up and expressed our needs. We had the experience of being labeled hormonal, as opposed to hearing the compassionate words we longed to hear: "Atta girl! I'm amazed by all that you do…"

Having expressed ourselves, we laugh out loud and declare for the entire world to hear how fabulous we think we are. Quietly, a bond forms between us; we recognize in each other the familiar symptoms of emotional depletion. As we continue to walk along, we stop here and there to take in the breathtaking beauty that surrounds us. Occasionally, we listen to the silence.

Finally, we relax into ourselves, each one of us happy to have found a like-minded traveling companion.

Book One

BE BOLD

In the cellars of the night,
when the mind starts moving around
old trunks of bad times,
the pain of this and the shame of that,
the memory of a small boldness
is a hand to hold.
—John Leonard—

1

Reclaiming a Piece of Your Heart

OMEN HAVE A blind spot. Although cognitively in tune, most women, contrary to what they might believe, falter when it comes to being in touch with their authentic emotional needs.

Through thirty-five years of being in private practice as a psychotherapist, I know that many women feel selfish, instead of emotionally empowered, if they give themselves permission to take up space in their own minds and honestly express their authentic needs. The truth is that women are hidden in plain view from themselves under the role: the cloak of caretaker, fix-it-all mom to all. Because nurturing is innate to most women, they unconsciously over-identify with the role. Often, they believe that who they are and the role of caretaker are one and the same, which of course is not true.

The oversight thwarts their ability to openly feel and communicate their deep-felt needs. The needs I'm talking about are the ones you have difficulty sharing, like asking for help or

You can't do what you want until you know what you're doing!
—
Moshe Feldenkrais

support when you really need it, when you feel vulnerable asking. The needs I'm talking about are those you somehow don't feel entitled to experience—the needs you avoid showing because you want to avert conflict. Because of this oversight, women fall prey to the number one paradox associated with the art and discipline of change: In order to be authentically, emotionally, open and available, you need to see where you are blocked; hence, the blind spot.

To See More Clearly, Change Lenses

Unfortunately, the lack of clear perspective creates a fault line in any template of change you might endeavor to create. Unless you shift perspectives—like you might attempt to change lenses in a pair of glasses to see better—any effort you make to care for yourself is limited. The truth is, you can only expand and develop as far as your cognitive thoughts, your head, can carry you, which is a far cry from what your heart offers you in terms of emotional support and intuitive guidance. For emotional self-renewal to take hold, you must get out of your head and into your heart. For this shift to occur, you need to be willing to see the world from a much gentler perspective, one in which the needs of your heart matter. To care for the emotional needs of your inner woman, who has her own set of heartfelt priorities apart from those of the caretaker, you need to create and negotiate a paradigm shift that lands you at the top of your priority list instead of last, or not on the list at all.

Take Back Your Heart!

The shift to create a mind-heart connection is two-fold. The change is paradoxical because you first have to learn to see with the eyes of your heart what you don't currently see, which is the difference between the all-consuming role of emotional caretaker and the emotional needs of the authentic inner woman. Second, to connect with your authentic core, you need to access the compassionate energy of the feminine experience so you can expand beyond the hard-driving masculine frame of reference that can stifle your soul when it is the only lens through which you observe the world. Ultimately, the only way for emotional self-renewal to occur is to have a felt emotional experience of shifting, as opposed to cognitively thinking your way out of your head.

In other words, you can't *think* your way into your heart; you have to *feel* your way into your heart, which is what your journey is all about.

Live Like You Matter

To LIVE LIKE you matter, you need to believe from the inside out that you matter. You actually want to experience deep in your gut a heartfelt knowing that you truly make a difference, which brings up conflict and confusion for some. Do not mistake the difference between inauthentic entitlement and the grace that comes when you know you are meant to take up space in the world and you are meant to be here beyond the role of über-nurturer of others. Ultimately, to feel authentically whole, you need to have a deep-seated confidence and down-to-the-bones knowing that you are here as a woman with rights and a destiny that only you can choose to fulfill.

There is no doubt that when you seriously commit to a journey of becoming, your world will be transformed for the better. Along the way, however, you will be challenged. As you get back in touch with yourself, you will have moments of feeling lost and confused. This is normal. What is also true is that with each piece of heart you reclaim, you will feel empowered to stay on the path of your own unfolding, your personal journey of transformation.

Awake Flat on My Back *(author's story)*

Sometime in your life you will go on a journey. It will be the longest journey you have ever taken. It is the journey to find yourself.

—

Katherine Sharpe

"CALL THE PARAMEDICS," was all I could utter to my best friend, Christine, who leaned over me as I lay motionless on her hardwood floor. Time stood still. Then I heard a male voice say, "You haven't suffered a stroke." *Thank you God*, I thought, my prayer of gratitude. It was five days before my birthday, the day I was going to turn it around, again, "take better care of myself." I guessed that my body had run out of fuel and wasn't going to wait for me any longer. As the ambulance rushed to the hospital, I experienced a strange peace and surrendered. *Now I can rest*, I thought. Always the therapist, I couldn't help but think, *How sick is that?*

Exhausted, I turned off all thought and dove deeply into the core of my being to fight off the nausea in my stomach and the dizziness that was still swirling around in my head. It was three days before I would open my eyes and not see triple, and five days before I would leave the hospital with a diagnosis of severe vertigo. During that time, I wrote a personal inventory of the decisions I'd made that had gotten me into this predicament. I cried tears of self-compassion as I became aware of how little I allowed myself to be nurtured by my husband and friends. I forgave myself, and apologized to my body, in particular, for not caring for myself the way I cared for others. Then and there, I committed to changing my priorities. No more giving lip service! I had to take the actions necessary to experience transformation.

My stomach cringed and my heart fluttered at the thought of admitting to myself that I wasn't as strong as I thought, and that I would have to start exposing this truth to others if I was to ask for and receive the support I obviously needed. I knew that as a self-reliant woman, dependency was my blind spot, my stumbling block, and the issue I would track as I moved forward.

Finding the Other Half of Your Soul: The Living Spirit of Feminine Energy

IF YOU HAD asked me before my crisis if I knew how to access the nourishing feminine energy within, I would have confidently said yes. As far as I was concerned, I could ask for help. I could set strong boundaries when needed. Yet there I was, flat on my back, helpless. I began to wonder. I began to have a dawning awareness that just because I could speak articulately about emotional self-care did not mean I knew how to actively practice self-nurturing, especially when what I wanted or needed might cause an inconvenience for someone else or interfere with a nice moment I was having with my husband. *What had happened? How could I think I was so open when in fact I wasn't?* Ultimately, my inquiry created a small inner schism, a crack in my self-perception. I thought myself to be a nurturer full of heart when in fact I was a walking, talking head disguised behind the mask of an emotional caretaker.

The schism within me widened during another moment of deep insight when I grasped the idea, "Why, even my self-nourishing activities are embedded in a masculine perspective." My meditation, yoga, and mindfulness practices were all part of a goal-oriented regimen I rigidly held in place. As I contemplated the paradox, I let myself experience how disconnected I was from the other half of myself: my heart, my soul, the expression of feminine presence within.

Gradually, I began to accept the truth that the masculine and feminine aspects of my nature were not in harmony, not in sync with each other, as I had previously thought. Quite the contrary, I was emotionally compartmentalized, split down the middle and didn't even know it. All because I could talk a good game. Yet I was considered high-functioning by all who knew me, including myself. What a lie!

As I lay in the hospital bed, I imagined how I might begin the process of opening up so I could create a bridge between the masculine and feminine states of my being. As I gave in to wonder, I felt myself expand internally. I savored the clarity of my newfound insight. Uncovering and facing my blind spot brought with it incredible freedom. At least now I could see the problem. How to heal the inner rupture would take time and a shift in priorities.

The Touch That Opens Windows of the Heart

I DIDN'T HAVE to wait long. The initiation of my journey began after talking with a couple of resident doctors, one in particular. She was Indian, and the embodiment of feminine energy. One night, she lovingly took my hand and placed it in her palm. I soaked in the heat of her healing energy. My body relaxed. Once she saw that I had settled down, she gently asked me to tell her about myself. As a result of my newfound insights, I decided to practice trust. I opened my heart. I told her of my fears, some I didn't even know I had until I started talking. I shared with her the story behind the mountain of emotional responsibility I carried and never thought twice about.

When I was done, she said, "My dear, you need to care for yourself the way you care for others. I'm sure those who love you will understand." Right then and there, I promised the beautiful young woman with soft, dark-brown, compassionate eyes that I would do what she was asking of me. I would learn to nurture myself, heart first. As I drifted off to sleep I imagined the beautiful woman to be the ambassador of the neglected aspect of myself, my inner woman. Thus began my journey to wholeness.

Running on Empty

THE NEXT DAY, lying in bed, I gently acknowledged how disappointed I was with myself for not listening to the body signals that had warned me to slow down, to stop and take a breather. I had been running on empty but hadn't wanted to admit it. There was always one more commitment to keep. I tuned out the inner and outer voices of love and support that had encouraged me to rest. I didn't hear them, or didn't want to hear them. I was self-reliant. As far as I knew, I was doing fine. As for the needs of the inner woman, her voice was not exactly one I was used to giving attention! Until now, I thought that balance meant keeping equal percentages of time for relationship, work, socializing, and exercise. Fortunately, without too much damage, my body was showing me otherwise!

As I left the hospital, I kept alive the rifts of wonder that had surfaced. I wanted to explore how I could strengthen the new bond I had formed with the gentler side of my nature. I knew that to fortify my emotional core, I would have to rethink my attitudes of self-reliance, which were now code words for hiding behind the mask of caretaker. To build a relationship connection with my authentic inner woman, I would have to let go of fear and open up and trust. Mostly, I would have to learn how to tolerate feelings of emotional vulnerability if I was ever going to flourish and develop a holistic, loving relationship with myself. The task would be a daily endeavor! As you can imagine, the decision to no longer deny or dismiss the authentic needs of the inner woman brought with it seismic eruptions, both in my heart and in my household. After all, how convenient is it when the person you are living with, even when it is just yourself, has no emotional needs for support?

For now, this is where my story leaves off and your exploration of wonder begins.

Point of Initiation

I ENCOURAGE YOU to think about opening up within. Take a moment to imagine expanding beyond the role of emotional caretaker. Imagine reaching within to connect with the authentic needs of your inner woman. How do you envision bonding with the softer side of your nature? Would you consider the idea from a healing perspective, or would you imagine the experience to be purely self-reflective, or be more about building emotional core strength? There are so many possibilities.

The world is round and the place which may seem like the end may also be the beginning.

—

Ivy Baker
Priest

THE BEAUTY OF WRITING

As YOU GIVE in to wonder, enjoy the sensation of opening up within. To enrich and deepen your state of wonder, just follow along. Allow yourself to be taken care of as you are gently guided through the set of three consecutive writing experiences below.

The intent of the first writing exercise is to help you expand within as you crystallize the connection you are forming with your inner woman. The writing prompt is an invitation to your unconscious to give voice to the thoughts, feelings, and images that lie just below the surface of your awareness.

1. Write Your Heart Out (Journal Writing)
Theme: *Insight/Inspiration*

PREPARATION
- Please take a long, deep breath. Then let it out slowly.
- Feel your body, your self, relax.

Write freely from the following prompt. Let the words flow. Do not worry about spelling or grammar. Even if what you write doesn't make sense, do not edit your writing. Always keep your focus forward. Never stop to read what you have written. The forward motion helps you open up and move beyond your intellect.

Prompt: She woke up inside of herself to…
Write in your journal for about three minutes.

Great! Now take a moment to contemplate what you have written.

1a. Write Your Heart Out (cultivating resonance)
Theme: *Insight/Inspiration*

The intent of this exercise is to help you connect with any insights that may have surfaced during your writing. The purpose is to give your opening-up process a personal focus.

PREPARATION
- Take in a deep breath. Let it out slowly.
- Settle your mind.
- Orient your attention toward what you have just written.

Describe below insights gleaned from your writing.

_____

_____

_____

_____

You already have the precious mixture that will make you well. Use it.

—

Rumi

Beauty Metaphor
For a beautiful, clear complexion, first cleanse the blemishes!

Lavender Notes
By recognizing when you go off track, you are able to change course with more ease. Of course, you can indulge yourself for a moment and consciously give in to running away, which, like a mini-vacation, can bring reprieve. The key is, however, to take responsibility for yourself and not blame others for what you are unable to do for yourself.

The Blame Game

I DON'T KNOW about you, but I have to admit that every now and again, I find myself in a little pocket of blame. For a very brief moment in the hospital, while feeling sorry for myself, I turned to blame. I had thoughts like, *If I ate better, blah-blah-blah! If I hadn't had that one cup of coffee, blah-blah-blah! If my husband, blah-blah-blah! If I had taken longer vacations, blah-blah-blah! If I weren't so darn self-reliant, blah-blah-blah! The bottom line is, blah-blah-blah.* Fill in the blank.

2. Write Your Heart Out
Theme: *Negative Thoughts*

The intent of this exercise is to give you a *felt experience* that the impact of blame has on your overall well-being, your physical body, clarity of thought, as well as your emotions. In the future, use the felt experience as a marker, a flag to let you know you are traveling away from your heart as opposed to toward it.

PREPARATION
- Through your breath, bring yourself into a state of mindful awareness.
- Elongate your spine as you center yourself in your body.

Articulate below those blah-blahs. Give in and have a sweet little pity party for yourself. Think of all the people, situations, and circumstances you want to blah-blah-blah about.

_____

_____

_____

_____

_____

Done? Feel better? I have to admit, blaming others can feel so good. After all, who wants to surrender to feelings of powerlessness and admit responsibility when it's so much easier to heap the problem onto someone close? Unfortunately, projecting your issue onto someone else is a short-term solution to a long-term problem. The truth is, being upset with yourself is what's usually on the other side of blame!

A little lipstick, if you please!

Congratulate yourself on allowing someone to care for and notice you: YOU. The truth is, your inner woman is juicy, delicious, and definitely worth taking time to know.

Inner Glamour Tips
Brighten up your day by savoring the idea of caring for and noticing yourself.

- Allow your intent to care for yourself melt your heart.
- To capture the essence of savoring, take a tiny piece of chocolate and let it melt in your mouth.
- Experience each nuance in flavor as the chocolate softens, changes texture.
- Imagine this is how you will experience the process of unfolding and opening up within.
- Each stage of becoming will reveal something a little wonderful about you.

Outer Glamour Tip
Make it your mission to find a shade of lipstick that complements your complexion. In other words, find a shade that looks great on YOU instead of following the fashion trend.

I live by a man's code designed to fit a man's world. Yet at the same time I never forget that a woman's first job is to choose the right shade of lipstick.
—
Carole
Lombard

2

Believing is Seeing

Y OU CAN'T OBSERVE what you can't see. Keeping the idea of emotional caretaker in mind, let's take a look at another task associated with your self-renewal journey. The purpose is to find and then reconnect with the original authentic landscape within you. For example, who were you before you consciously, or unconsciously, realized that to receive love and support, you had to care for others first? Possibly, you intuited you had to please, validate, and not bother those in charge of caring for you. What were you like before you experienced the role reversal?

Imagine your world when you intuitively knew, believed, and trusted that you could reach for and expect to receive the love and support you needed just because you needed it? Imagine the freedom of movement and expression of joy you experienced before you unconsciously created a defensive coping strategy to fit in with the family system you grew up in!

As you know from the story of my health crisis, I am self-reliant. The key question I had to ask myself is, what did I believe

15

would happen to me if I weren't so self-sufficient? What underlying belief caused me to disconnect from my authentic core rather than face the truth in front of me and acknowledge the dependency feelings I had inside of me? Cognitive awareness of what I needed to do did not actually help me care for myself the way I needed in order to be healthy. In fact, my smartness was my hindrance.

Developing a Discerning Eye

THINKING ABOUT WHAT you need to do to care for yourself is different than emotionally owning your authentic needs and believing you can act upon them with confidence and trust. To create a paradigm for emotional health, you have to unearth the limiting beliefs, the barrier within, which prompts unconscious defense responses. I like to think of the discernment process in the same way you might approach caring for a beautiful lawn when you have a gopher problem.

Like catching the gophers that wreak havoc on your beautiful lawn, you have to go deep within to find and then sort out how to get rid of the pesky, elusive, limiting beliefs that keep you walled off and out of a loving relationship with yourself. To accomplish the task, you have to learn to see. For example, you have to know the difference between when a mound of dirt is signaling a gopher is present and when the mound of dirt is actually a divot, possibly caused when Grandma used your lawn as a putting green when she was visiting. Otherwise, you risk tearing up your lawn for no good reason. In the same way, you have to know when your coping strategy is healthy and when it is not, because self-reliance is not in and of itself bad; often self-reliance is an asset. And you certainly don't want to tear yourself apart for no good reason.

My Story *(author's story)*

I AM A late bloomer. I have always been a few steps behind everyone else, or so it seems to me. I attribute my delayed development to the fact that when I was a young girl my family moved abroad, to Switzerland, to be exact. While there, I felt torn between two worlds, America and my best friends who I knew were enjoying hamburgers and fries, and my new life with my new girlfriends with whom I shared a daily snack of bread and chocolate. To stay connected to the teen scene I had left behind, I wore bobby socks like the American girls I saw when I rode the tram to Geneva, and nylons like the Swiss girls I went to school with in the countryside of Corsier.

Eventually, much to my chagrin, the American girls ignored me. My Swiss girlfriends on the other hand, who only wore nylons, took my strange style in stride. I had become one of them. I blended in. I loved it. I hated it. My confusion only deepened when my mother had a nervous breakdown and was sent to a sanitarium in the Swiss Alps for a couple of months' rest. Her absence cast a shadow over the inner rift I felt.

I was eleven. Overnight, the safe world of my mother's nurturing and loving presence was gone. To adapt, I became my father's little helper. I felt proud of the role. I felt special. I became emotionally self-reliant. Cutting myself off from my heart was my way of coping with the loss and pain inside me.

To take care of us during my mother's absence my father hired Marouscha, a rather quirky Russian nanny, with a receding hairline and translucent skin. I immediately became the mediator for and protector of my siblings from this waif like, strange woman who had bouts of crying when she thought of her homeland. I took to the role of caretaker like a duck to water. As I learned to straddle two worlds, the days unfolded magically. One

Since we can't change reality, let us change the eyes which see reality.

—

Nikos Kazantzakis

day I heard the words I longed to hear, "We're going home to America." I was sad and elated all over again, only this time in reverse.

Four years seemed to disappear in a blink. Our return to Southern California was as I imagined it, except for one thing. More than I was aware of, I had adopted some of the Swiss mannerisms, one of which was to be blunt with your best friends. Who else were you going to depend upon to tell you the truth about your looks and other pertinent information you needed to hear as a young girl if not your best girlfriends?

My foreign ways did not go over so well with my new friends. No one wanted to hear, as we gathered around the mirrors in the bathroom anxiously admiring ourselves, that yes, in fact, the blemishes you have on your face do deter from your looks but you are my friend and you are fabulous anyway! Suffice it to say, we worked through shock waves before best friendships were possible. The good news is I was a genuine novelty. I was so out of it, I was in! I made close friends and thrived. The rift inside me gently faded away, and all that remained was my fluency in French and some wonderful memories of the great outdoors.

I would not fully discover the impact of the role of pseudo-mother until years later when, as a psychology major in college, I became aware of my tendencies to control my emotional environment. Through therapy, I reconnected with my core self, the young girl I'd left behind so long ago. Much to my delight and amazement, she was still there in the shadows of my heart, waiting for my return. She was full of life, wonder, defiance, and love. The more I connected with her, the more I became one with my authentic self. Through the gift of self-compassion, I came to terms with the choice I unwittingly committed to so long ago. After a lot of angry and sad tears, I realized that what had been missing was a loving relationship with my authentic self. During the process, I had to come to terms with the truth that my self-reliance was a liability as well as an asset.

Between a Rock and a Hard Place

AFTER MY HOSPITAL experience I was not initially fully aware that my self-reliance was a coping strategy that had become a barrier. Yeah, I knew all about my control issues and could discuss them ad nauseam—which did not mean that I could experientially transcend what was holding me back. It wasn't until I started to put my emotional needs first that I became aware that I was not very familiar with what my needs were. Awkward, I felt like a trapeze artist flying through the air without a net. This was an unsettling experience, and I didn't like it.

I knew that if I did not shift my ways and learn to nurture myself, I could end up back in the hospital. So, between a rock and a hard place, I took a leap of faith. I began in earnest to explore the unconscious role and negative impact of the self-reliant coping strategy that had become my way of maneuvering through life. I was so surprised to learn the far-reaching impact that this seemingly benign approach to living had on my relationships!

The Paradoxical Giving Caretaker

HERE IS THE key: Until you find or revisit the beliefs upon which your inner child based her default coping strategies, you are held hostage, emotionally limited and stuck in time. The failure to connect with your positive, authentic core beliefs becomes an inner barrier that prevents you from nurturing and championing your-self successfully. In other words, how can you be the woman you want to be when a part of you is locked in a mind-set of caretaking, buried in childhood and motivated by an archaic need for emotional security, as opposed to sincere gestures of altruism for another? You can't.

Last to Know: First Step in Awareness

THE FUNNY THING is that, just like it is with everyone who has a blind spot, I was the last one to get it. I was so busy living from the perspective of self-reliance, not needing support, that I had no experiential awareness that I was part of the reason why my inner woman was depleted and upon investigation feeling emotionally neglected. Unaware of my strategy, I continued to be an emotional caretaker when my services were no longer required. Thus, the first step toward deconstructing the barrier within is learning to see when the state of self-reliance or other defensive coping mechanism, called your *character strategy*, is authentic and when it is used as a protective caretaking measure to keep you feeling safe.

Setting the Story Straight

IDENTIFYING HOW YOU look at the world through the lens of a default character strategy is humbling, to say the least. For example, self-reliance is wonderful when you are alone and need to take care of a few things. The coping skill becomes a liability when you stop seeing the support that is all around you. Harm is caused when, blind to your needs, you do not even see or experience the world as a safe place to lean. Instead, you turn inward and lean on yourself, which leads to a disconnected existence. Can you now see why I did not hear the loving suggestions my husband was giving me to take it easy the day I went to Christine's? He was kindly offering me support. He had my back. I just didn't hear it that way! I knew better.

Now, let's have you begin to discover the negative impact of your coping strategy.

THE BEAUTY OF WRITING

Lavender Notes
Like the discomfort of a pebble in your shoe, internal discomfort provides you with a clue that something is wrong. Investigation of what doesn't feel right helps you discern and then discover elements of your coping strategy that you can then repair and shift out of.

Self-Assessment Questionnaire

You will begin the discovery process with a self-assessment questionnaire. The intent behind the questionnaire is to help you discern the behavior patterns in which your blind spot might be lurking. Please notice how the questions below vary in tone and theme. The questions reveal tendencies and patterns commonly used by women to avoid connecting with their authentic core.

PREPARATION
- Take a deep breath. As you breathe out, center yourself in your body. Get comfortable.
- To get the most out of your experience, notice if you resonate with any of the patterns of behavior listed in the content of the question.
- Realize the questions are intended to provoke insight and invite curiosity, nothing more.

Ask Yourself

1. Have you wondered if you unconsciously get sick so you have an excuse to rest, as opposed to giving yourself a time-out because you are depleted and simply need to regroup?
2. To find comfort, do you turn to shopping or have an extra glass of wine instead of using your voice to ask for encouragement and support?

There are years that ask questions and years that answer.

—

Zora Neale Hurston

3. To feel worthy, do you hide in busyness or work instead of believing that you matter for who you are and not because of what you do, or produce?

4. To find ease and balance within, are you overly involved in your children's lives, as opposed to facing the emptiness, the pain, and anxiety, left in the wake of your children leaving home?

5. Are you waiting for something or someone to change so you can get on with your life?

6. Do you face the disappointments that come when life does not go the way you expected it to go? Or do you pretend you don't feel upset and use fantasy to escape?

7. Can you hear the difference between "doing" your life and "being" in your life?

8. Finally, do you know how to stay in a loving relationship when those you love cannot care for your emotional needs the way you want them to be cared for?

The Value of Vulnerability

If you are like most women who answered the questions honestly, you might feel exposed or vulnerable. Please stay in touch with the feeling of vulnerability, as opposed to trying to get back in control. Resist the temptation to analyze or explain away any resonance you might feel with the question(s) you identified with. Also, you don't have to like how you are feeling to know you are on the right path. The truth is, I hate feeling what I falsely consider needy or weak. I like feeling in charge and self-reliant. I'm really good at it. Fortunately, through the painful wake-up call I shared with you earlier, I realized emotional vulnerability is strength rather than weakness. By default, I learned that the only way to get in sync with my heart was to let go of my false self, my Ego, and the part of me that I thought was open when I was not.

Beauty Metaphor
Compare the state of vulnerability to a luxurious moisturizer: A little goes a long way.

3. Write Your Heart Out
Theme: *Self-Assessment*

Let's use the unresolved issues identified in the questions above to help you flush out the emotional experience you might be missing due to your original disconnect. Below are needs commonly covered up by inauthentic caretaking behaviors, or thoughts of escape.

    If you were to guess, circle the need below that best identifies a need you yearn to have filled?

Safety Love Recognition Trust Rest Self-Worth

We can't take credit for our talents. It's how we use them that counts.
—
Madeleine L'Engle

Lavender Notes
As you might let a wonderful antique you rescued from your grandparents' attic take up room in your home before you decide what you want to do with it, so let the need you identified take up space in your heart.

A little lipstick, if you please!

Inner Glamour Tips

Owning a heretofore, unrecognized need requires the emotional capacity to make room for the need that is being recognized. To get used to the idea of taking up space, please let the activities below represent, like a space-saver indicates your name on a dinner party table, the need you will be reintegrating into your life over the course of our journey together.

> *I appreciate subtlety. I have never enjoyed a kiss in front of the camera. There is nothing to it except not getting your lipstick smeared.*
>
> —
>
> Hedy Lamarr

- Set a beautiful vase out on the table.
- Go to the florist and buy a magnificent flower.
- When you come home, carefully put the flower and some water in the vase you have set aside.
- Treat the delicate flower with care and tenderness, as it represents your vulnerability, a part of you that you want to learn to see and get to know.
- For a mind-body connection, realize this is how you want to treat the part of you that is opening up.
- Like the flower drinks in the water, take in the idea that you are special and worth caring for.

Outer Glamour Tips

- Treat your lips with care.
- Keep them moisturized.
- For this purpose, choose lip balms over lip gloss.

3

Ski the Volcano

ELF-REGENERATION BLOSSOMS when you heal old wounds, hurts, which, until they are dealt with, cause simmering frustration and or possibly anger that keeps you stuck in the past. This is especially true when the activity of healing is addressed in a frame of forgiveness. To find strength of heart, you have to be willing to take full responsibility for where you are and how you got here. Sorry, there are no shortcuts around this truth. Believe me I've tried every avoidance tactic I could think of and more, but to no avail! I'm sure you've done the same to escape looking in the mirror and saying, "Okay, kid, it's do or die time!" Let's not delay any longer. Let's get to the task of looking within!

In this chapter, you will explore the intensity and quality of any anger you feel so you can transcend where you find yourself in this moment. By looking at Mother Nature, you will get a glimpse of how the heat of anger can lead to the possibility for renewal.

Let's now take a look at Mother Nature to see how this might work.

We must embrace pain and burn it as fuel for our journey.
—
Kenji Miyazawa

Witnessing a Firestorm *(author's story)*

*You've got to find
the force inside you.*

—

Joseph Campbell

I WAS STANDING on the beach in Marina del Rey, California. It was a warm autumn evening. Smoke filled the air and burned everyone's eyes. The beach was crowded with onlookers, all gazing in silence in the same direction toward the mountain ridge to the north. The blaze that had been raging for days in the Malibu brush was spreading and starting to crest the hills, moving toward Topanga Canyon. A halo of yellow, magenta, and orange lit up the sky and crowned the silhouette of the Santa Monica Mountains. The ethereal glow seemed to herald the flames that were on the move. I'll never forget the collective gasp as the first few flames flickered over the mountaintop and began to eat the homes of friends and strangers alike. We all wept quietly. A couple of hours later, thanks to a shift in winds and the perseverance of courageous firefighters, the fire turned around and went back up the hill in another direction. Many prayers were answered that night, as whole communities were able to go back home.

The aftermath of Mother Nature's fury left the mountains charred black and without shrubbery. The smell of smoke filled the air for weeks. As I drove up the beautiful California coastline to see the damage that was done, I lamented the loss of the beauty of the mountains I so loved. Seeing the sight of charcoal mixed with sand and dirt was overpowering. The ghost of the fire was a felt experience I could see in the sight of the frames, the shells of houses burned to the ground. Witnessing the sole homeowner going through the rubble of her memories was heartbreaking, eerie, and daunting. What to salvage and what to leave behind was all part of the process. How would life ever come back to normal?

Miraculously, the next spring, an unforeseen event occurred. The hills came back ablaze with bright colorful wildflowers and new green brush. It seems that the intensity of the fire's heat was just the right temperature to pop open seeds that had been dormant for hundreds of years! Mother Nature taught us all a lesson. Out of trials of fire, possibility is born.

Lavender Notes

When you engage in emotional process work, you always want to have a frame of reference for the work you are doing. In terms of personal growth, the idea is to feel the feelings to get to a place of relief beyond, which is different than stuffing your experience to get it over with.

THE BEAUTY OF WRITING

4. Write Your Heart Out
Theme: *Commitment Contract*

You can't see and change what you don't face. The path to possibility is often through pain or upset. Let's process some of the upset contained in the story of your awakening or insight so that you can let go and start fresh. The work you are about to do will be addressed in stages.

To start, let's have you commit to letting go while keeping an eye on the seeds of possibility contained in your current self-awareness process.

PREPARATION
- Take in a deep breath and let your mind go.
- Are you ready to leave the past behind?

CHECK ONE
___ Yes, I am ready to leave the old behind.
___ Not so sure I'm ready to leave the past behind.

Learn to see, and then you'll know that there is no end to the new worlds of our visions.

—

Carlos Castaneda

Fire, Forgiveness, and Follow-through

THE FIRST MOMENTS of self-reckoning are not fun. Quite the contrary, like noticing a bright red blemish that shows up on your face to attest to last night's French fries, facing the consequences of poor choices can bring forth feelings of self-disgust and anger. Believe it or not, this is the moment when change is possible. Different from the toxic feelings associated with the "blame game," upset feelings are normal when you hold yourself accountable for less than stellar behavior. The feelings often emerge when you decide to mend your ways and seriously commit to change.

When you begin the renewal process, everything inside of you shifts. You experience a sort of death of the coping habits that went before, which brings out all sorts of emotional, stormy weather. There is nothing you can do about the upset; it is part of the letting go/moving on process. So, like finding shelter to wait out a summer storm, you must patiently hold a space within yourself and wait for your feelings to pass.

Beauty Metaphor
Compare the work you are about to do to a facial exfoliation/beauty scrub, or a face peel. Imagine how fabulous you will look and feel on the other side of the pinch of discomfort. Of course, the treatment you are having has a lot to do with the intensity of the experience you are undergoing. The section below is for those of you who feel like you've just had a face peel as opposed to an exfoliation or light beauty scrub.

Feeling Your Heat/Anger

To LOOK AT what is being asked of you, let's go back to the Malibu fire I just described and see what you can learn from the firefighters about containing fire. From where I stood on the beach, the fire appeared as if it was burning out of control. The truth is, the firefighters were on the job. They were aware of every move and fluctuation of the fire. They knew the location of each new hot spot. They did not just let the fire burn out of control, willy-nilly. Through awareness, they created a plan for eventual containment of the fire. To achieve their goal, they brought in helicopters with fire retardant and sprayed it over the fire. They put boundaries, a perimeter, around the fire so they had an idea of where and how they were going to attack and contain it. They also cleared away brush, fuel, so the fire would have less chance of gaining ground. Each move was gauged according to the strength of the fire in that particular location.

You can apply to your feelings the same approach the firefighters used to contain the wildfire. With mindful awareness, you can tune inward and notice where your anger/upset is located in your body. Taking a moment to look closely, you will discern the quality of the anger. For example, is the anger static, pulsating, or is it expanding? Is your fire hot, or has it turned cold? With the information you gather, you have, like the firefighters, various options for managing the intensity of emotion you have around the particulars of your circumstance.

To contain and thus feel safe with your upsetting emotions, it helps to acknowledge the intensity of your feelings. So your feelings do not spill out into your life and cause pain to those you love because of your lack of conscious awareness, it is important that you own your feelings.

I'm sure you can relate to a moment in time when a sudden spurt of upset, somehow before you knew it, found its way over the threshold of your lips just because you had feelings smoldering inside of you that you could no longer contain.

Creating a Perimeter/Boundary, Around Upset

THE SECTION BELOW is mostly for those of you who are going through a difficult moment and feel angry with the realization that you have to change. If, however, you do not find yourself in such a circumstance, think back to a moment when you felt cornered and had to give in and shift. So that you may participate and gain awareness of your coping patterns when it comes to anger, utilize your previous moment of upset as a frame of reference for the following.

*You must do the
thing you think you
cannot do.*

—

Eleanor Roosevelt

5. Write Your Heart Out

Theme: *Intensity of Emotion Scale*

The purpose of the exercise is to familiarize you with the process of checking in with yourself so you can create a plan of action to cope with your emotions.

PREPARATION *Use your body as a tuning fork.*
- Take a deep breath and let yourself relax.
- Focus in on any upset you feel. Think about how you might rate your feelings.

*What if we
smashed the mirrors
and saw our
true face?*

—

Elsa Gidlow

Rate and record the level of your intensity:
1 (very mild) through 10 (filled with rage)
I would rate the intensity of my experience at _____.

The questions below are intended to support exploration, as well as help you continue to expand awareness of the nuances found in your place of disconnects.

Self-Awareness Questions
(To help you identify patterns of avoidance)
1. Do you avoid listening to advice given to you? *Now you know you have to listen.*
2. Are you mostly in such a hurry that you do not pause long enough to consider the alternatives available to you? *Now you know you have to slow down.*
3. In escaping from a situation, do you find yourself jumping from the frying pan into the fire? *Now you know there is no escaping and you have to face the music.*
4. Are you too intimidated to ask for what you need and thus lose opportunities? *Now you know it is a greater risk to not ask. You know you have to risk asking, no matter what.*

5. Are you feeling so defeated that you have stopped engaging? *You know you have to keep going in spite of the possibility of rejection.*

6. When you are in a good space, do you hesitate bringing up an issue out of fear rocking the boat? *Now you know keeping quiet does not work in the long run. You know you have to risk speaking up regardless of how well things are going.*

In the same way that you identified the intensity of your emotion above, you now have the opportunity to clarify the quality of the upset that pertains to patterns of avoidance. As it was with the firefighters, your knowledge will assist you in knowing what type of boundary or perimeter to put around feelings of upset. That way they will not spill out all over everyone.

6. Write Your Heart Out
Theme: *Self-Assessment/Anger Nuances*

PREPARATION
Tune into yourself and relax.

Draw a circle, a boundary around the description that best mirrors the quality of the upset you experience when you realize you have to let go of control to open up and change.

Mildly Irritated   Simmering   Frustrated

Irritated Angry   Boiling Over   On Fire   Enraged

Take a moment to look at the word you circled. Notice what it looks like to have a boundary around your emotions, like a perimeter around the fire.

Lavender Notes

Going forward as you process the material, make sure you have a boundary around your experience. You want to be able to feel feelings without being overwhelmed by them. The way to ensure you do not become swept away by your feelings is to mindfully be aware at all times that you can set boundaries around your feelings, which is different than squelching your experience.

Expect a Miracle

IT's OKAY TO feel angry when you are upset. Open acknowledgment of how you feel is one of the first steps toward self-renewal and healing. When you work in an authentic manner, the Mistress of the Universe always seems to come out and play.

True Story *(author's story)*

AFTER I GOT out of the hospital, I became very aware of how intensely angry I felt. I was changing—more precisely, having to change—my ways. More than the irritability that comes with coffee withdrawal, I knew that I was on fire. The commitment to shift gears in my life was having an impact. My determination to change was fuel for the fire inside of me. With every step toward my new way of being, I felt a tug/yearning to take two steps backward. The inner struggle sparked some of the deepest upset I've ever known. I could literally feel myself being torn apart, causing a rift between my old self and my new self. I didn't like it. I so wanted to give up and go back to my old ways, go unconscious.

On a particular Saturday morning, I was observing the fact that "I really have a short fuse." To keep peace in the household, I decided to warn my husband about how I was feeling. I went into his office and said, "Honey, I just want to alert you... I am feeling really angry. As a matter of fact, I feel like a volcano ready to explode. So, please, give me some room (notice how I was asking for space) if I act a little edgy." I had never expressed myself so graphically before. He just looked at me and said, "Okay."

Not quite knowing what to do with all the anger I was feeling, I decided to see if I could walk it off. I went back to tell my husband what I was doing and that I would be back in a couple of hours. I drove to the spot where I would start my walk, got out of my car, and started down the familiar path alongside a beautiful Venice canal. Feeling comforted, I turned inward.

I wanted to see how and where my body was holding the anger. Upon exploration, I realized what the expression "beside myself" meant, because that is exactly what I was experiencing. I felt like I was outside of myself—literally beside myself walking with myself—and I was angry. *A little disassociated, perhaps?* I mused to myself. Just then, I felt the presence of another walker behind me. As he passed, I caught a glimpse of a message on the back of the stark white T-shirt he was wearing. There in big, bold, black letters were the words, "Ski the volcano!" I could not believe my eyes. The laughter that rose up from deep within me quelled the edges of the anger I had been feeling. *Well, at least someone is listening,* I thought as I began to ponder the origins of the mysterious message I received.

A Mind Map to De-Stress

LIKE A MOTHER holds an upset child, hold all of your upsetting experiences with love and compassion. The activity keeps you in tune with the part of yourself that is struggling, on fire. To share with you the nuances of what I was doing when I took my walk, let's review the list of activities I was accomplishing while staying in relationship with myself.

I knew what I was upset about. I was upset at my circumstances. To contain my upset and keep my relationship with my husband intact, I creatively communicated to him what was going on within me without analyzing the inner turmoil.

I set out to exercise, knowing movement helps reduce agitation and anxiety. I kept open and vulnerable to the upset within me. To stay present I kept describing to myself how and where I was experiencing the upset in my body, which is a handy little tool I learned through sensorimotor trauma training. The "naming and describing" exercise reconnects you with yourself and starts to soothe you when you are in a state of distress.

I gave space for possibility. Because I was in tune and present, I saw the synchronicity in the humorous message that presented itself to me on the back of the walker's shirt.

I followed the path of letting go by allowing the spontaneous laughter and wonder take over and quell the inner fire.

I stayed open and wondered about the invisible world beyond. I did what I could do and no more. I framed the whole process in a perspective of letting go, as opposed to digging for more insight and information.

Although not a happy camper, I knew in the end all was right with the world. I ultimately gave meaning to the whole experience by concluding, *I must be on the right path—heading right down the slopes of that volcano!*

Let's reconnect. Let's go back to our imaginary walking trek we began a while back, and see what mischief we can stir up.

Our Story: Imagine...

By now we are fast friends. We've spent a day or two together climbing hill and dale! On this sunny morning we're having a lovely cup of tea, listening to our guide lay out the day's itinerary. Our destination is a natural, spring-fed pond with a beautiful waterfall. We look at each other with a smile that says, "Sounds like fun. I'm in." Then we hear the words, "The hike is a bit of a challenge. To get to the springs, you have to climb over some rocks." The guide then looks directly at us and says, "It will be hot and dusty." "How dare he imply...," we say, feigning insult, as we become even more resolved to go on the voluntary hike.

Four hours later, our T-shirts and faces drenched with perspiration, we begin to wonder. Suddenly you catch a glimpse of what looks like an azure pond ahead. Spirits renewed, we climb over the last couple of rocks to find what looks like a spectacular mirage, except that it is not. We strip down to our bathing suits and plunge in. *Ah!* The water is tepid, not cold as expected. After a couple of moments of shared mirth, we feel drawn to go off in our separate directions to commune with nature in our own private way.

You notice a shape beneath the surface of the water, a dark rock that could double as an armchair. *What a find!* you tell yourself as you glide onto warm stone. Your butt firmly settled on the seat of your throne, you lean back and listen. You feel fabulous, sensuous, one with nature's song. As the sun caresses your face, you notice your attention turning inward. Quietly, you realize how good it feels to be you! You bathe in the glowing realization that you love the woman you know yourself to be. You let out a deep sigh. You hear an inner voice say wisely, *Out with the old, in with the new!* Inspired, you commit to forgiving yourself for the ways you've betrayed yourself. You luxuriate in how good it feels to be at peace with your decision.

After a time, you open your eyes, which are mysteriously drawn to a message scratched into the rock above the waterfall: "Ask and you shall receive." *No coincidences here*, you muse.

On impulse you swim over to the waterfall. Before you know it, you find yourself standing under nature's outdoor shower. As you experience the cool water bearing down on your scalp, you find tears rolling down your cheeks. You imagine each tear holding the story of a little transgression against yourself. You realize how many times you neglected to put your needs, yourself, first. As your salty tears blend with fresh water, you relax. You feel renewed. You let out a huge sigh that comes from somewhere deep down inside of you. You let go and suddenly imagine the upset within you being washed away. Mesmerized, you relish the experience of feeling yourself becoming lighter and lighter.

From here you know, in a deep, knowing kind of way, that you can move forward. You imagine the feelings of your authentic self, the woman within, becoming a priority in your life. Feeling restored, you recognize it's time to get out of the water. You swim to the edge of the pond and gracefully make your way to a private patch of grass where you placed your fanny pack earlier in the day. Inspired by the words "Ask and you shall receive," you take out your journal and, in a final gesture of letting go, you decide to write a heartfelt letter to yourself.

To be continued...

Lavender Notes
It is common for whole conversations to take place between the old and new parts of you. Often, a beautiful merging of the two voices takes place toward the end of the writing. The dynamic is conflict resolution in action.

Ask and you shall receive.

—

Proverb

7. **Write Your Heart Out** (Journal Writing)
Theme: *Insight/Conflict Resolution*

PREPARATION
- Imagine yourself under the forgiving showers of the waterfall.
- If the waterfall spray could talk, what words would the spray say to you as it caresses you? Or, if you want to come at the experience from another perspective, think of the part of you that most needs to receive a loving embrace. Focus in on that part of you. *Start by writing down what you might want to say to the part of you that is yearning for special attention.*

Tip: When I do a workshop I will set aside a half hour for the cumulative writing. You may want to keep some tissues on hand. If you find yourself crying, keep writing through the tears!

Prompt: Dear… *(fill in with your name)*

Remember: For an imaginative experience, write in the first person as if you are the voice of the waterfall encouraging you…

Write for three minutes (in your journal), or for a half hour as if you were in a workshop.

Beauty Metaphor

After having a facial, you are instructed to stay out of the sun to protect your new skin. To protect the beautiful place you have just cultivated inside, be gentle with yourself.

7a. Write Your Heart Out *(cultivating resonance)*
Theme: *Insight/Conflict Resolution*

PREPARATION

- Take in a breath and tune into yourself.
- Become aware of consciously connecting with your voice.
- When you feel ready, read what you have just written out loud.
- When you are finished, underline the word(s) or sentence you resonate with the most.

Please record your resonant sentence below.

_____

_____

> *Forgiveness is the fragrance the violet sheds on the heel that has crushed it.*
>
> —
>
> Mark Twain

What is Done is Done

YOU HAVE JUST completed some very important work, which is to face any anger, frustration, or irritation you may be experiencing and let it go so that you may focus on the future. In doing so, you finished one of the intents embedded in the journey of Book One, which is to cognitively connect you with the prospect of opening up rather than fanning the flames of any upset you may be experiencing.

Keep in mind that the journey is about moving beyond and opening up forward. At this point, you are invited to gently let go of any self-recriminations you might be experiencing, and face forward toward the future.

A little lipstick, if you please!

*Lipstick is really
magical.
It holds more
than a waxy
bit of color, it holds
the promise
of a brilliant smile,
a brilliant day,
both literally and
figuratively.*

—

Roberta Gately

Inner Glamour Tips

1. To protect the wonderful, loving experience you are giving yourself, set a boundary around the work you have just done.
2. Imagine placing a pretty, colorful ribbon, or a tastefully sculpted iron railing, for more protection, if needed, around your heart. Always turn away from any impulse or behavior that wants to draw you back into the past. Consciously turn a deaf ear to the choir of inner voices that will no doubt chant songs of guilt. Keep in mind that the voices of fear are outdated, like dry skin. They have done their job. Give them a blessing of gratitude, brush them off, and refocus.
3. Scrub a floor if you must, to dissipate the energy contained within a destructive impulse. Make sure you move and let the feeling pass through you.
4. Keep your focus forward on the light of truth where the spirit of the authentic feminine holds you whole and beautiful.
5. If you recall, in the last chapter you used the flower as a space holder for your feelings. Let the vase that contains your flowers act as a reminder that it is okay to set boundaries.

Outer Glamour Tips

1. For a lipstick experience, glance through a fashion magazine and notice shades of lipstick. From bright red to the palest pink, notice which lipstick represents the woman you feel yourself to be in the moment.
2. For fun, do this a few times to see if your experience shifts.

4

Beyond Belief: Dancing in Moonlight Magic

IF YOUR SELF-RENEWAL journey is to be more than a reconfigured balancing act, it is important that you transcend your defense mechanism, go beyond what is familiar to develop the softer side of yourself. In this part of the book, as you shift into the feminine experience, you will be shown what it looks and feels like to suspend old beliefs, while new beliefs have time to come into view. As you proceed forward, you will be asked to take a leap of faith to go deeper within, to descend into the inner pool of "knowing." The endeavor is tricky because you cannot approach the task of going within with your usual paradigm of thought; otherwise, you will fail!

Let's compare the journey you are about to take to that of learning how to swim. At first, while the instructor explains water safety rules, you may sit on the edge of the pool in your dry bathing suit. Then, there comes the point when you have to jump into the water and get wet!

It is good to have an end to the journey toward, but it is the journey that matters, in the end.

—

Ursula K. Le Guin

The intent of this chapter is to help you experientially recognize through immersion the realm of the feminine. To play in the pool of the mysterious feminine, you are invited to finally say, "I don't know what getting into the water will be like, but here goes." To delve into the feminine experience, you need to take, as opposed to talk about, a leap of faith.

Ultimately, to feel secure living with the feminine part of your nature, you want to tune into yourself and trust, even though you might not be able to make logical sense of what you are feeling, or being led to explore. To open up within, it helps to be curious about the coincidences that occur between the issues you are contemplating and the messages and insights you receive from what seems like out of nowhere. The synchronistic dance between the internal and the external experiences, between the known and unknown awarenesses, is exquisitely subtle. You might compare the experience to watching a woman do a dance of veils. Now you see the dancer, now you don't. Sometimes you are the dancer; sometimes you are the veil.

The ephemeral dance of veils reminds me of taking a walk in moonlight. To see what is in front of you, you allow yourself to be drawn in. You relax your focus, set a softer gaze. You slow down. With every shape that emerges out of the shadows, you refocus. You learn to see with your heart and listen with your soul.

In the same way, to enter into the world of the feminine, trade in harsh judgment for keen discernment. Follow flow and let go of force. Trust faith and let go of uncertainty. In the hearth of your heart, let the strength of masculine energy be present without sucking up all of the air in the room. To nurture yourself, learn to look and see differently. Become familiar with your senses of sight, sound, smell, taste, and touch. In fact, allow yourself to become immersed in sensuality.

Trust that most of the time, even though you do not have concrete answers at your fingertips, you will be shown your next step. To receive the intuitive gifts associated with the feminine, learn to see with different eyes and listen with different ears. Paradoxically, to get in touch with your deeper self, get curious and cognitively step aside for a moment so life can unfold. Tune into the mysterious unknown and go beyond…

Go Farther *(author's story)*

I FELT STUNNED. "What do you mean I can't stay at your home?" I was speaking to one of my best friends, Barbara. I had called, excited to tell her I had just booked my trip back East. We were finally going to see each other face to face. I couldn't wait. Then Barb told me she had decided to put me up at an inn so she would have more time to practice the piano before the recital I was to attend. As I sat on the phone digesting the information, I felt my temperature rise. I couldn't believe I was taking time off from work, flying all the way across the country, to be picked up by some driver and taken to some unknown destination in the middle of the night!

Finally, I got a grip. "Okay, then," was all I could say. After all, I didn't want to ruin the trip that was already in the works. Then, my friend said the words that mattered: "I knew if I picked you up, we would be up all night talking. I couldn't afford to do that to myself. You'll see, the place is beautiful." How could I argue with that?

On the date of my arrival, I was picked up by a driver and, in the pitch-black dead of night, driven to a country inn. In retrospect, the only thing I distinctly remember is the smell of cigarette smoke that greeted me as I climbed the creaky stairs to my room. The next morning, to escape the fumes, I decided to take a walk. As I strolled through the beautiful property that sat on the bay, I came across a wooden post on the side of the road. I sat down. *What a weird beginning of a trip,* I thought, feeling my aloneness. *Maybe there is a reason I have been brought here to this place.* A couple of minutes later, I felt a pull, a sort of tug in my chest. It was as if something from across the little road was trying to get my attention. *Odd,* I thought, taking a closer look.

You have the power in the present moment to change limiting beliefs and consciously plant the seeds for the future of your choosing.

—

Serge Kahili King

There amidst trees practically hidden from view was an old stone graveyard. The mysterious pull continued. "Okay, okay. I'll go see," I said to no one in particular. I crossed the street, trod through some tall grass to pass through a broken-down wooden gate. I stood at the entrance of the cemetery, waiting to see what would come next. "Over here" came the soft, mysterious whisper. Thus summoned, I walked over to the largest black-gray, cracked headstone in the graveyard.

I stood in front of the stone and read the inscription: "Here lies Henry Gray, 1834–1885. He brought his family to Fairfield, Connecticut. He was part of the Unqua tribe of Indians." Then just below the engraving were the words, the message that gave me chills "*Unqua* means 'Go Farther'!" *Are you kidding me?* was all I could think. *Exactly how much farther am I supposed to go?* I lamented. To regain my emotional center, I decided to put my talking head aside. With a gentler focus, I turned inward and wondered: *Truly, how much farther can I possibly go?* At that moment, I couldn't imagine what it looked like or felt like to "go farther." I had come as far as I could possibly go—at least in my mind. Intuitively, I understood I was way in "over my head." I was in the realm of the mysterious, the sphere where Indian guides show up and point the way.

Later, while waiting for Barbara on the porch of the inn, I rolled over in my mind what "go farther" could possibly mean, when suddenly I caught a glimpse of violet passing through the trees. Before I saw Barb, I heard her music. As she came around the corner, I heard Aretha on the radio belting out the words "Respect yourself." *Yes!* I thought, amidst howls of laughter. I knew I had received the clue I needed to head down the pioneer path of "go farther."

The funny thing about the story is that the event occurred as I was giving some contemplative thought to what it meant to live in the spirit of the feminine. Upon hearing the words "Respect yourself," I felt as if I were sitting on the edge of the pool in a brand new bathing suit "looking good," wondering how I was going to get wet while keeping my pool allure, when suddenly I was pushed into the water. Problem solved. I had to deal!

Mind Map: To Let Life In

You probably surmised from the story that I was taken off guard when Barbara shared the news of her change of plans. She knew it and I knew it. At that moment, a few decisions needed to be made. The first decision was to decide how I wanted to be in relationship with myself. Could I center myself enough to let the feminine presence within guide me through the gauntlet of upset, or would I crash emotionally and give in to reaction? The second choice I considered was how to stay in relationship with my friend while being true to myself. Was I going to keep her close or push her away because I was hurt? I have to admit, putting on my therapist hat for self-protection was really appealing. Yet I knew that hiding behind my professional demeanor would turn my friend into a client and compromise our friendship. Then, there was the pièce de résistance, which was to unleash the bitch within to dish out a lovely portion of guilt. I could almost taste the long, juicy, tedious discussion we could have about how let down I felt. The truth was, I held a lot of personal power in my hands.

To steady myself, I created a fourth choice, which was to pause so I could respond, instead of react and spout. I took a deep breath and focused. I remembered to let life in! I connected with my commitment to be open, vulnerable, and emotionally present while in relationship. My whole body relaxed. The release brought forth the awareness of another promise, which was to always be curious. My intentions allowed me to reframe the unforeseen detour into an adventure full of expectation. All I had to do was to keep an open heart and say *yes*.

Living Dual Realities

As you may have noticed, my experience/quest was not linear and logical; it was nonlinear and at times illogical, at least from the masculine perspective. However, the open, intuitive state of mind allowed me to suspend judgment so I was able to hear and respond to the mysterious call coming from the cemetery. Curiosity led me to the headstone. The practice of faith helped me believe that the message "Go farther" was a gift meant for me. I perceived Aretha's words "Respect yourself" as a wink from the Mistress of the Universe that all was well and good.

Feeling the Magic: Finding the Movement

You ALSO HAVE the choice to cultivate the feminine within. To do so, permit your-self to let go of control and be surprised. When you find yourself at the farthest edge of what you are aware of, and can tolerate, take one more step. Be willing to suspend what you know so you can step into the unknown, and thus "go farther." To soothe yourself, bathe in the reflecting pool of the feminine. When you do, notice all the different options and outcomes available to you. Realize that you actually have the gift of choosing your life experience!

THE BEAUTY OF WRITING

8. **Write Your Heart Out** (Journal Writing)
   Theme: *Inspiration*

   Let's delve into the unknown so you can swim in the waters of your feminine. Put the analytical/cognitive part of you to the side for now. Get curious and open up to the unknown.

The tradition of pilgrimage is as old as religion itself.

—

Dr. Lauren Artress

PREPARATION
- Take a breath. Let it out very slowly. *Be aware of what it is like to let your breath out slowly.*
- Notice your posture. Are you sitting comfortably in your chair? Is your spine straight? Are you facing forward or leaning to the side? Are the soles of both your feet securely planted on the ground? *When your posture is centered and you are sitting up straight, you access more...*
- Take another couple of breaths. Release and notice your body relaxing. Notice your shoulders softening. Notice your breath becoming even. *Stay connected to your body as you...*

- Drop into your heart, the part of you that holds the mysterious, the awe and pool of feminine energy within. *You are energetically multi-tasking, becoming more fully present.*
- With your heart open, prepare to receive a message from your writing. *If you recall, I believed I would receive answers to my questions if I allowed myself to be open....*

Be fearless in your desire to explore. Write from the prompt below. Include your senses. Write uncensored for five minutes.

Prompt: She looked into her heart and saw the words: "Go farther," which she ...

Write in your journal for three minutes.

Moonlight, Magic and Movement

IF YOU LIKE control, the prospect of hanging out in the unknown is scary and anxiety producing. During the process you may uncover the belief that you will die if you let go. Paradoxically, at the moment you think you are a goner is when you arrive. When you feel most vulnerable is when you are home, in the space of your inner belonging, where the authentic essence of who you are resides and is most powerful.

The feminine is the birthing place of life. An implicit rule of evolution: When something is born, something dies. So the idea that you might think you could die, or might be dying as you let go and open up, is somewhat true. To emerge into your authentic self, you cannot hang on to the old, that which makes you feel safe; to feel whole, you have to expand beyond and allow yourself to become. It is nature's way, the way of life. To experience grace, learn to live with the dual reality that holds both light and dark, cycles of birth and death, the old and new. If you think about it, whether you like it or not, you are engaged in the process of saying goodbye and hello.

The key is: Develop an emotionally flexible and adaptable inner space. Let the space be one that cradles all aspects of who you are, the part of you that is letting go and the part of you that is becoming new.

Lavender Notes
The capacity to hold opposite experiences simultaneously requires strength of heart and clarity of mind. Both are skills that help you cultivate a loving relationship with the woman within.

See with the Spirit of Your Heart

To DEVELOP STRENGTH of heart, be true to yourself. Let yourself face and see what you see as well as feel what you feel. When you open up to the mysterious and hold the moment as sacred, instead of trying to analyze it to death, or letting someone else interpret your experience, the regenerative spirit of feminine presence will come to your aid. Your willingness to look anew is the only invitation the Mistress of the Universe needs to propel you into new spheres of living. The unimagined is a place where you hold the experiences of loss and gain with love and acceptance, with detachment and belonging.

So you can have a felt experience of what I'm describing, let's turn again to Mother Nature, who has the capacity to both fascinate and devastate simultaneously.

True Story *(author's story)*

DENALI NATIONAL PARK in Alaska is a natural preserve where grizzlies amble about, deer and elk run free, and moose roam the tundra. The park is a place of beauty and extraordinary wonder. Yet the beauty holds a difficult, dark truth to absorb. While chugging along in the yellow school bus, on a very narrow road that leads to a small summit from which you can see Mount McKinley in the distance, I heard the guide utter the words, "Only the fittest survive here." I gasped to myself as I looked out the window into the face of a large grizzly bear eating grass by the roadside. *Who makes it and who doesn't?* I pondered. The guide continued: "This is a natural preserve. We are not allowed to interfere with nature, even if it means whole populations of animals come close to extinction!" I felt respect, dread, and awe course through my veins. I experienced the power, majesty, and awe of life and death living side by side.

I can still feel the revelation of that moment. I felt the pulse of life in the palm of my hand and in my heart. I'm hoping you grasp the awe and the mystery found in the question: Which animal lives and which animal dies?

In addition, I would like to draw your attention to the way each tourist was asked to respect and view/witness the philosophy of the preserve. In the same way, as you delve into the waters of the feminine (yes, the swimming pool metaphor is still relevant), hold the mysterious found in the core of your nature sacred. As Aretha reminds us, "Respect yourself." Leave the essence of who you are alone; you are naturally, authentically beautiful.

Beauty Metaphor
You are being asked to stretch. To avoid stretch marks, take it slowly. Do not hurry the process. Be gentle with yourself. Savor opening up from within.

*To putter is
to discover.*

—

**Alexandra
Stoddard**

---

*See without
looking,
Hear without
listening,
Breathe
without asking.*

—

W.H.Auden

9. Write Your Heart Out (Journal Writing)
Theme: *Contemplation/Self-Respect*

The purpose of this writing experience is to help you contemplate your truths of becoming. Now, let's find out what the word "self-respect" means to you.

Preparation
- Please take a long, deep breath.
- Allow yourself to experience the sacredness of life.
- Place your hand over your heart. Quietly say the words, "I respect myself." Pause.

Using the prompt, write in your journal for three minutes. Be sensuous with your descriptions.

Prompt: Hearing the words "respect yourself" resonate deep within herself, she…

9a. Write Your Heart Out (cultivating resonance)
Theme: *Contemplation/Self-Respect*

To get the most benefit from moments of insight, give yourself time to savor your experience.

Preparation
(Please read all the way through before implementing)
- Take a moment to relive the experience of your writing.
- Create a conscious connection with yourself through your breath.
- Read your work out loud as you stay in relationship with yourself through your voice.

- See if, in your writing, there is a direct message of what "respect yourself" means to you.
- When you are done reading, take a moment to underline the message(s).

Record the sentence or word(s) you underlined on the line below.

_____

_____

Let Nature Take Its Course

As YOU COMPLETE the journey of awakening set aside for you in Book One, be aware that as you open up, some parts of you will wither away while other aspects of you will blossom. Ultimately, as you learn to flow with the natural cycles of life and death, you will find harmony and learn to trust the chaos you must sometimes endure to find peace.

A little lipstick, if you please!

Mother Nature is a wonderful teacher. She holds all of her mysteries with such elegance. You also have your mysteries, the issues that disturb you and the assets you cherish. Let's continue to have you learn how to sustain and cultivate the power of the feminine experience, the essence of who you are.

A little lipstick, a little paint make a woman look like what she ain't.

—

**Dottie Perry
(95 years young)**

Inner Glamour Tips

- Today as you drive, walk around, or sit outside, notice something in nature that inspires you.
- Observe the transitory nature of two worlds living side by side. For example, you might notice a leaf on a tree ready to detach and fall. You might notice a dark barren branch with a hint of green heralding spring. Or you may see a sparkle of sunlight dancing on a wave in the ocean.
- Whatever season you find yourself in, look at how the cycle of birth and death are one and the same, about life.
- Please find your own way to meditate upon the experience you have chosen to contemplate.
- Realize you are beautiful and exquisite....

Outer Glamour Tips

- Protect your lips from the sun by using a lip balm with at least SPF 15.
- If your lips are chapped, use medicated lip balms. The good news is lip balms have the best consistency for keeping your lips looking youthful!

Book Two

BE BEAUTIFUL

And the day came when the risk

to remain tight in the bud

was more painful

than the risk it took to blossom.

—Anaïs Nin—

5

When Seeing Is Everything

YOU CAN'T "DO" relationship. For a relationship to flourish, you want to "be" relational. Therefore, the ability to discern when you are in a *cognitive state of doing* and when you are in an *experiential core state of being* is of the utmost importance, especially when your goal is to create a heartfelt connection with the feminine experience within. Paradoxically, the simple act of admitting to yourself when you are not emotionally open brings you into a state of being. When you can non-defensively say to yourself "I am not open" is when you are fully present, open and emotionally vulnerable, barrier and all. From your vantage point, inside the realm of the feminine, you often experience, before you can see, the wall that blocks the path to your heart. You are positioned to go deeper within.

Continuing to use your innate curiosity as your guiding light, you can examine the barrier/wall for fissures, weak spots. Through your effort you will come to see aspects of your

The eyes
of my eyes
are opened.
—

e.e. cummings

caretaking behaviors that are not authentically motivated. Once identified, the fault lines can be tagged as entry points for further self-reflection and discovery, which is what this chapter is all about.

Blind Spot, Barriers, and Character Strategies

I LIKE TO compare the process you are about to engage in to the puzzles you find in a children's game book; specifically, the quizzes where you are asked to find various items camouflaged in a picture. At first, when you look at the picture you see nothing. Everything on the page seems like one big drawing. Yet, as you shift your gaze and look more closely, you are able to decipher here and there the items you are looking for. Perhaps it is "a key" that unlocks "the door," and so on. As you may recall, when you find one item you are looking, for it's easier to spot the others. Once you put a couple of items on your list of answers, you feel victorious, like you cracked the code.

You are on your way. Similarly, you are now going to look in the direction of your blind spot to find clues to help you identify the character strategy that makes up and is in fact your inner wall.

As you proceed forward, allow yourself to be curious and courageous. Make sure you keep the faith even when you face truths you do not like admitting to yourself, like when you realize that your most cherished personality asset is also the liability that defeats and deadens you at the very core of your being.

As I mentioned earlier, self-reliance was my prized asset, even though, to my surprise, it was also the blind spot that kept me out of relationship with others. Now, it's your turn. You are being asked to go deeper within to expand the sacred space of the authentic feminine. As it is with the directions in the children's book, you will be given a heads-up to see what to look for as you walk the path. For support, I invite you to recall "Our Story." If you remember, the guide asked us if we wanted to go on the voluntary hike to a beautiful pond. We were warned in advance that the path would be a challenge. Fortified by our bond of friendship, we said, "Yes."

Alone in a Crowd of Two *(author's story)*

FLASHBACK MANY, MANY years. *I knew I shouldn't have risked it,* I admonished my twenty-something self as I sank into a metal chair, barely able to breathe. The screaming pain coming from my sciatic nerve was back in full force. I wasn't sure how I would make it to my car with the heavy package I was holding. *I'll ignore the pain and deal with the consequences later*, I told myself, determined to carry on.

By Los Angeles traffic standards, I was a long way from home. I had been shopping in a mall, in the Valley. I lived on the Westside, another world away. As I sat there amidst all the people scurrying about, I wondered how I was going to get into my little yellow Toyota without going into further spasm. The thought of having more spasms made me flinch. I took the only Tylenol I had in my purse and waited. Finally, I was able to move a little, I sprinted as fast as I could to my car. Getting into the car was as painful an experience as I had predicted it would be. However, true to my nature, I proceeded home through sheer force of will.

Later, while I was lying on a heating pad in the living room of my Brentwood apartment, the phone rang. It was my best friend, Geri. I had known her since grammar school. We were catching up. I told her of my experience. There was a full moment of silence before she spoke. "Why on earth didn't you call me? You know I live right around the corner from the mall." "Why would I?" I answered, truly perplexed. "Because I'm your friend, and I would want to come and help you out!" she said in a hurt voice. I was stunned. The truth was, I had not even thought about reaching out for help. I was so self-reliant that the idea that I might "need" help did not even cross my mind. In fact, having needs was not on my playlist. Young as I was, however, I knew enough

When we look into the mirror we see the mask. What is hidden behind the mask?
—
Mandy Aftel

to know I had discovered a blind spot. The pain and astonishment in my friend's voice woke me up.

At that moment, my cognitive self-awareness journey kicked into full gear. I committed to change. I was determined to think about reaching out for help. I didn't realize that the part of me that needed to reach for help was where the blind spot lived. I didn't know that admitting to having emotional needs for support was the unseen "barrier within." I did not realize until way later that the issue had to be addressed while in relationship, not outside of relationship. I had no idea that in a healthy relationship it's natural to actively seek out, emotionally depend upon, and expect support from those closest to you. Not because you are in a crisis, but just to make life easier.

Trending to Failure Without Knowing It!

As WITH OTHER defense strategies, the self-reliant strategy blinds you from acknowledging that you have emotional needs. The denial runs so deep, you don't even relate to yourself as a person who has needs. From that point of view, how could you possibly know how to reach out when you need help? As seen in the story, you don't even recognize that there is anyone around to give you support, much less ask for it! When you are blind and can't see, you literally can't see. Again, coming from the perspective of the self-reliant strategy, the overriding idea is that there is no one to lean on. The core belief that you are on your own stems from an original experience felt in childhood.

In my case, when my mother became ill, I unconsciously and consciously realized the seriousness of the situation. I realized intuitively that it was up to me to sink or swim. The way I chose to cope was to swim. I chose to curb my emotional needs for nurturing to avoid being a problem for my father, who I could see was overwhelmed, and to help my siblings, who were younger than I was. The choice was simple. As I mentioned earlier, I liked the idea of being the strong one, the one you could rely on. I liked the feeling of being in control. It wasn't until I was in the hospital, later in life, that I got a glimpse of the liabilities found in the strategy of self-reliance. I then realized as wonderful as it is to be a self-starter there is always another side to the story!

Beauty Metaphor

To invest in the appropriate skincare product and implement a nourishing skincare routine, you need to know your skin type. For example, is your skin oily or dry? To get the best quality of care for your skin type, it's important to answer your aesthetician's questions as honestly as possible. Otherwise, what's the point?

To keep it light, compare the work you are about to do with identifying your skin type.

THE BEAUTY OF WRITING

10. Write Your Heart Out
Theme: *Self-Assessment Character Strategy*

So far, I have only mentioned the character strategy of Self-Reliance. There are, however, three other character strategies. They are the Go-Getter, the Sweet Talker, and the Grin and Bear It. You are now going to identify your character strategy.

Here's a little heads-up: When you read through the descriptions below, you may identify with more than one strategy. There is, however, one strategy you will resonate with the most. To discover your dominant strategy, answer the questions below as honestly as you can.

You need only claim the events of your life to make yourself yours.

—

Florida
Scott-Maxwell

PREPARATION
Use your body as a tuning fork to help you discover the strategy you resonate with.

- Take a deep breath.
- Center yourself in your body.
- Feel the ground beneath your feet. Breathe.
- Lengthen your spine.
- Let your chest expand upward and a little outward in a gesture of receptivity.
- Relax your jaw.
- Relax your neck and shoulders. Breathe.
- Relax your arms and your hands. Feel the tip of your fingers letting go. Breathe.
- When you feel calm within your mind-body connection, proceed.

Read the list of selections below a few times before answering. Circle the number that best describes you.

1. You are a very busy taskmistress. You have a lot of irons in the fire. Your mind tends to race. You strive for perfection. You fear failure! You yearn for calm and inner peace, yet you avoid sitting still because it tends to make you anxious.
2. You like having people like you; most people do. Charm is your mask. You aim to please. You have difficulty expressing your needs directly. You tend toward flightiness. You have a hard time keeping commitments. You strive for approval. You yearn for recognition. You fear rejection.

3. You have a capacity to endure. You sacrifice and put the needs of others before your own. You believe that if you express your need for freedom, time out for yourself, others will get angry. You tend to worry and may feel hopeless. You feel trapped, like a martyr. The words "Yeah but" are your trademark. You yearn to let loose and feel light-hearted.

4. You have a lot of emotional strength. You hate the idea of being weak or dependent. You would rather get a job done by yourself than waste time including, or "bothering," others. You have no patience for girly girls and/or being coy. You tend to turn inward instead of outward when upset. You fear feelings of vulnerability. You tend to be intense. You yearn to be nurtured.

Hidden in Plain View

Each description of the behavior patterns above has an embedded story of childhood. The story holds the unconscious motivation behind the behaviors found in each of the character strategies. You will use the information above to begin deconstructing the barrier within. Ultimately, you will use what you learn to reinforce a self-nurturing renewal program.

FYI: This program addresses the missing needs of the part of you that did not have those needs met when you were a child, before your character strategy became your default way of relating.

Now, let's take a look at the character strategy that defines your defense mechanism. Again, keep in mind that you may see qualities in yourself that relate to more than one strategy. Only choose one.

If you chose description:
Number 1 ………your strategy is called **Go-Getter**
Number 2 ………your strategy is called **Sweet Talker**
Number 3……… your strategy is called **Grin and Bear It**
Number 4……… your strategy is called **Self-Reliant**

Lavender Notes
Hold the strategy you identified with love and acceptance. Notice what happens when you slowly read each word in the description of your strategy.

Can you see the busyness and striving in the words **Go-Getter?**
Can you see the foxiness in the words **Sweet Talker?**
Can you feel the heaviness in the words **Grin and Bear It?**
Can you see the self-centeredness in words **Self-Reliant?**

Depending upon the strategy, can you begin to imagine what experience a child might have been faced with in the home environment to make the decision to choose a certain character strategy/coping tool above the others in order to fit into the family/relationship system?

I tore myself away from the safe comfort of certainties through my love for truth —and truth rewarded me.

—

Simone De Beauvoir

11. Write Your Heart Out (cultivating resonance)
Theme: *Self–Expression Character Strategy*

Now, let's take a moment to have you express how you feel about the character strategy that defines you best.

PREPARATION
Take a breath and tune into your power of observation.

In a few words, write down your initial impression of what you felt when you read the name of your character strategy.

Start Here:

_____

_____

Behind the Looking Glass

Now let's take a look at what issues are found in each character strategy so that you may get a clear idea of the part you need to reclaim.

Go-Getter

On the good side, you are very achievement and task oriented. You are successful in most of the endeavors you undertake. You are the information go-to person. You are highly thought of for your energy and the way you tackle tasks.

The issue here is that your work is never done. Because of the inability to feel complete, you can't stop. There is always more to do. You never fully connect with feelings of satisfaction. Because of this difficulty, you have trouble experiencing the inner peace you crave.

The people closest to you feel they are never enough, or can never do enough to satisfy your level of perfection. Your hurried attitude makes it difficult for those around you to feel like they can give you the support you ask for. Although you like cooperative efforts, it may not be very gratifying to cooperate with you.

Sweet Talker

On the good side, you are a person who is charming, gregarious, and easy to like. You have a quick smile. You are fun to be with, sometimes considered the life of the party, although you might not feel that way.

The issue here is that you feel invisible. You are so busy focusing on charming others that you do not stop and think about what you might like. In fact, you may not even know the sound of your own authentic voice. Your desire to please leaves you feeling depleted and under-appreciated.

The people closest to you can never say enough to make you feel worthy. Additionally, your lack of directness makes you hard to read. To avoid conflict, and maintain your likeability factor, you may fib a little here and there, which causes a lack of trust with those closest to you.

Grin and Bear It

On the good side, you are a giver. You are always looking for ways to nurture others. You are witty, although possibly a little gritty in your humor. Those closest to you can count on you when you give your word.

The issue here is that you sacrifice your playfulness and freedom by feeling overly responsible for others. Interestingly, you simultaneously tend to blame others for your unhappiness. You are full of complaints and yeah-buts. You long to let go but won't give in and surrender to what you desire most, freedom of expression. Your long-suffering nature makes it hardest on *you*! You, therefore, feel frustrated in your relationships.

The people closest to you have a hard time giving you support. You interpret constructive criticism as an all-out personal attack. You wait for the other shoe to drop. You have difficulty hearing how people appreciate what you do for them. Your pessimistic demeanor makes it hard for those around you to share in moments of delight and to see the light that shines within you.

Self-Reliant

On the good side, you are content with your own company. You are a self-starter. Caring for yourself is second nature to you. Because of your self-sufficiency, you are easy to take places because you have so few needs.

The issue is, you are an emotional loner. Your fear of dependency prevents you from seeing all the support that surrounds you. In truth, you do not perceive yourself as someone who needs help, when at times you do. Unfortunately, your lack of self-perception closes you off to ideas that do not originate from you. You tend to be intense, although the cheery exterior you display initially hides this fact.

In your relationships, the people closest to you find it difficult to feel needed or important. Your intensity makes it difficult to connect through play; although, when you are in the mood, you will play. Those closest to you may not feel seen or valued. When they pull away, you may not be bothered because you are happiest being left alone—which, of course, is the opposite of what being in relationship is all about!

Seek What Is Hidden

As YOU MAY have noticed, all of the strategies have one theme in common: hiding the authentic self. When you pause and observe closely, you begin to see the wall that needs to be bridged to find your way back home to your heart. You can actually begin to imagine a template for change. For example: What type of change would you suggest for:

1. **The Go-Getter, who has difficulty just being?**
   She believes she will finally find rest when all is done, which paradoxically will never happen because she is not focused on completion, she is focused on being industrious. She sees the world through eyes that are always looking for the next project!

2. **The Sweet Talker, who has difficulty being direct?**
   She believes she is invisible and is not worthy. Therefore, she never sees or hears the acceptance and/or recognition she is given because, paradoxically, she is too busy striving for it. She sees the world through the lens of a popularity contest.

3. **The Grin and Bear It, who has difficulty playing?**
   She believes that if she takes a break from enduring the burden of others, they will get angry. Her fear of upsetting others paradoxically keeps her upset and out of sync with herself. She sees the world through a lens of drudgery.

4. **The Self-Reliant, who has difficulty being nurtured?**
   She believes there is no one around to lean on. She never lets herself get into a position of vulnerability, so she does not have to see herself as weak and admit she has needs. She sees the world through a lens of self-sufficiency.

Can you begin to see what I mean when I say that, when you are in a defended/protective state, you really can't see what you don't see? What makes it difficult is that with a blind spot, you don't even know where to start looking!

Before I built a wall, I'd ask to know what I was walling in or walling out.

—

Robert Frost

12. **Write Your Heart Out** (Journal Work)
Theme: *Insight/Wall*

You can't see what you cannot observe! In the next piece of process work, you are creatively going to familiarize yourself, through drawing, with aspects of your character strategy, your barrier, your blind spot. To soften the emotional impact of the work you are about to do, let's call on the energy of the feminine to support you as you draw and face your inner wall.

PREPARATION

To experience the nurturing presence of the mysterious feminine, visualize yourself sitting outside on a nice warm summer evening. All is right with the world. You let out a huge sigh and feel yourself relax into your body. Your mind is calm. You notice a hint of salty ocean breeze or lavender in the air. You feel peaceful. From your place of tranquility you notice a wall you had not seen before. You take a closer look. Is the barrier a wall of rocks, a wooden fence, a barricade of trees and flowers? You wonder, is the barrier there to keep you out or to keep someone locked away? You let your imagination go and in your mind draw a picture of the wall and the story it holds.

Draw a picture in your journal of the barrier that stands between you and your authentic self. Remember to be descriptive and sensuous. Think of your character strategy and what it would look. You may even use graffiti on your wall if you like. Take five full minutes. Learn to take up space!

Take a moment to pause. Allow the work to soak inside of you.

True Story *(author)*

ONE WOMAN IN a class I was teaching shared the picture of her barrier. On her paper she had painted what looked like two colorful walls with a wide blank space between them. The whole class was fascinated. "How is that a barrier, when there is a hole in the wall?" one woman asked.

"Well," the woman said coyly, "the place where you see blank, I actually painted white. You see, my barrier is invisibility. You think I'm open and easy to reach, but I'm not. Actually, I don't ever let you see me!"

12a. Write Your Heart Out (cultivating resonance)
Theme: *Insight/Wall*

Every wall communicates a message. Sometimes the message is loud and clear. Other times the message is subtle. In all cases, the type of wall communicates the intent of the person who built it. Let's find out what your wall communicates about the intent you had when you built it many years ago!

PREPARATION
- Take a deep breath. Center yourself.
- Take a look at the picture you drew of your wall. Let yourself intuit what the wall is saying.
- If the wall could talk, what would it say to you?
- What message does the wall send to others?

The problem is how to be open enough and safe enough at the same time.

—

W. A. Mathieu

Jot down some of your thoughts if you like. Or, for more impact, go straight to the drawing of your wall and write the words on the picture of the wall itself. Or do both. Remember, seeing kick-starts believing!

_____

_____

_____

_____

Every Story Has a Picture

THERE COMES A time when you want to bring all of your awareness into focus. To help you, let's briefly return to our imaginary journey.

Our Story: Imagine…

WE HAVE RETURNED from our hike. Now, alone in your room, you revisit the day. *What a day*, you muse, thinking about how we had climbed over boulders and such. Smiling, you recall seeing yourself and me in a less than dignified light. Slowly, you realize that, with each grumble that was uttered as we made our way to the pool, we became closer friends. No more standing on pretense. We had let down our guards. We now knew each other, warts and all. We were adventurers. In spite of all the trials and tribulations, we made it to the pool and back! We dunked ourselves into the sacred waters and came out renewed.

Unfortunately, on the way back, we ran into the same boulders that brought up the same old issues: feelings of inadequacy, blah-blahs, and such. The feeling of peace was lost. Even a shower didn't bring back the state of tranquility you experienced earlier. You wonder. *Where did all the peace go? What is it about me and my issues that gets in the way and limits such magnificent experiences?*

To restore the feeling you had at the waterfall, you ponder what you need to do to circumvent the issue, the barrier within.

The first thing you decide is to love and respect yourself, no matter what. Flaws and all! You decide to continue to open up, which you now know means facing yourself. You remind yourself that self-renewal is linked to releasing the innate beauty within. Drawn inward, you begin to wonder what it would be like if you were to let your inner beauty shine, pierce the wall.

As you drift off to sleep, you see a woman. She looks like a wiser version of you. Slowly, she turns to face you. She gently taps the seat next to her and says, "Come, sit here beside me. I will guide you inward." You see yourself finding the place beside her. As you turn to look at her, you see that her eyes are full of love and light. You notice a piece of paper and a pen on the desk in front of her. She glances toward the blank piece of paper as if to suggest that you start writing. Receptive to her guidance, you pick up the pen and begin.

To be continued…

---

13. Write Your Heart Out (Journal Writing)
Theme: *Wisdom*

Tap into your creative unconscious to find out what is below the surface of your awareness.

Preparation
Take in a breath and align your body.

Using the prompt write whatever comes into your mind from the perspective of the wise woman.

We are made wise not by the recollection of our past, but by the responsibility for our future.

—

George
Bernard Shaw

Prompt: Imagine the Wise Woman whispering in your ear that, to return to the sacred garden within, you only need to…

Write in your journal for three minutes.

13a. Write Your Heart Out (cultivating resonance)
Theme: *Wisdom*

PREPARATION
- Take a moment to read out loud what you have written.
- Please read slowly so you get to know the sound of your own voice.
- Underline the words or sentence you resonate with.

Record the words you underlined on the line below.

_____

Wonderful! You have traveled far within and connected with your inner wise woman. This may be a good moment to check in with your body. To integrate your work, fortify your mind/body connection.

Settle into New Skin
Notice the impact your new awarenesses are having on you. See if you notice any shifts taking place within. Let them occur. Stay with them until they settle. Do not try to analyze. Just be present with what is taking place. When you feel settled, take a final breath. Let the beautiful work you have done take up residence in your heart. Imagine the Mistress of the Mysterious Feminine close by, smiling at all that you are becoming.

A little lipstick, if you please!

Now it's time to restore yourself. To connect with the softer side of your nature, you want to develop an awareness of the essence of your feminine presence.

Inner Glamour Tips

1. **For the Go-Getter woman:** What's a girl to do if she has nothing to do? See if you can rest and take a break. When your mind starts to rush, just say to yourself, *Hey, I am doing something: I'm learning to do nothing but rest.*

2. **For the Sweet Talker woman:** Speak up and notice how no one faints! Don't be afraid if your self-image isn't in place. Your light naturally shines from within without any effort on your part.

3. **For the Grin and Bear It woman:** Notice how many yeah-buts you utter and how this stifles conversation as well as wastes your time and energy. Save the fight for when you really need it. Develop the strength to accept, as opposed to quickly dismiss, the support being given to you by those you trust or who have your best interest at heart. To shift out of the yeah-but response, focus on the pleasure or relief found in the suggestions being offered to you.

4. **For the Self-Reliant woman:** Notice how often you decline invitations from people who offer you support. Learn to say yes to someone who is offering support whether you need it or not. You might even say yes to the grocery clerk who is offering to take your groceries to your car. Practice what it feels like to be a princess!

> *Beauty to me is about being comfortable in your own skin. That and a kick-ass lipstick.*
>
> —
>
> Gwyneth Paltrow

5. **For all:** Tonight, when you lie down to rest, pay special attention to your eyes. Refresh your eyes by gently covering them with a cool fragrant eye pillow. Let the darkness and beautiful aroma soothe you.

Outer Glamour Tips

1. To make 50+ lips look younger, choose creamier lipstick and avoid matte or gloss.
2. Younger than 50? Make sure you wear liner under your gloss. It makes the gloss last longer.

6

Finding the Invisible

ELIEFS CAN RAISE you up or tear you down. Hidden, toxic beliefs, those you are not aware of in the felt sense of the experience, are the worst kind. Like stalkers who prey on the innocent, they lie in wait and strike when you least expect it. The most insidious beliefs are hidden right out in the open, in plain view, under the guise of caretaking gestures motivated by the need for self-protection. Like the rare sighting of a leopard camouflaged in the jungle underbrush, undermining beliefs are difficult to spot even for the most experienced eye. Until you know where to look for the limiting beliefs, you can't begin the task of deconstructing the wall that keeps you separate from your authentic self.

Nobody can conceive or imagine all the wonders there are unseen and unseeable in the world.

—

Francis P. Church

You Find What You Look For

ONE OF THE first tasks required to bring your authentic needs into focus is to notice how the dynamics in your family of origin influence your behavior and possibly lead you to unconsciously empower others instead of yourself. By seeking recognition, love, and self-worth outside of yourself, you leave yourself wide open to be manipulated by others and thus limited in your capacity to care directly for your own needs. Secondly, as a woman, you are naturally inclined toward the role of emotional nurturer, caretaker. Thus it is helpful to explore your instinctual beliefs along with cultural pressure to see how these thoughts influence you. For example, do you conform to the idea that to be successful you have to do it all? Or do you define your own measures for success? The idea is to be a nurturer by conscious choice, as opposed to succumbing to conformity. The combination of limiting beliefs presents quite a delicate operation to untangle and straighten out before you can successfully access the nurturing resources of the authentic woman within.

No wonder it's hard to find emotional balance! Without the right self-sustaining perspective, you are defeated before you begin. Paradoxically, the challenge becomes how to put *yourself* at the top of your priority list, when you are not even in the picture of your own life. Can you now see the value of exploring your unconscious mind-set to find the distorted lens through which you observe your place in the world?

Coming Full Circle to Begin Anew

BY CONSCIOUSLY MAKING the choice to connect with the woman within through a lens of love and compassion, as opposed to a "How can I fix me?" or "What can I do for you so that I can get you to give me what I need?" frame of reference, you have stepped foot on the path that leads you to your heart. You are opening up emotionally. So far, you have identified pitfalls associated with your character strategy.

You have seen through your drawing the nature of your inner wall. Now it's time to get to the root of the problem, which in this case is finding out why the barrier was erected in the first place; learning about the underlying belief that keeps you locked in the past.

Know Your Voices, Hear Your Self

WE ALL HAVE voices within us. Some voices encourage us, and others, which I like to call the guards at the gate or our talking heads, discourage us. Unless we learn to identify, befriend, and quell the voices that limit us, we are doomed to repeat patterns that fail. Without a well-founded capacity to identify the voices that seduce us away from our core self, we won't be able to discern between the voices that hurt us and the voices that support our endeavor to re-connect with our authentic self.

Like family, all voices feel familiar and, like members of a family, each voice has its own way of perceiving the world. The truth is that the part of you, the non-authentic voice, representing the guard at the gate, has her own way of looking at the world, which is to keep you safe from experiencing feelings of vulnerability, especially when in her mind-set, feelings of openness trigger hurt and/or shame.

Lavender Notes

When limiting beliefs are present, you live in the past. In fact, when it comes to buried limiting beliefs, it is as if time has stood still. Your perceived inner reality is the one that molded the beliefs to begin with. Most limiting beliefs are based in experiences that caused feelings of hurt, or lack of safety.

Having learned this, you can imagine the perspective from which your little girl, the guard, views the world. As you might guess, she looks at the world through the lens of danger, fear, and lack of trust. Armed with outdated information, she uses her voice to fill your ears with messages of worry and discouragement. You may have found some of those messages written on the wall you drew in the last chapter. Let's use your newfound wisdom and self-awareness to begin the process of shifting paradigms of fear into paradigms of trust, abundance, and hope.

Leap of Faith

The recurrent moments of crisis and decision, when understood, are growth junctures, points of initiation, which mark a release from one state of being and growth into the next.

—

Jill Purce

IN THIS PART of the book, to maintain openness and forward momentum, you are going to be asked to consciously make the decision to trust. No matter what type of mental interference your talking head may try to distract you with, please create the intent to keep your heart open as you move through the chapter. The purpose is to provide you with a cumulative experience of awareness that will allow you to create a shift in perspective. All you have to do is follow along to "go farther!"

Heads-up: During the informational parts of this chapter, let go and enjoy. Do not worry about absorbing all of the material. Take in whatever you can and leave the rest.

Fairy-Tale Practicality *(author's story)*

When I was a little girl, I used to be fascinated by the fairy tale "The Princess and the Pea." I couldn't figure out why the princess was so uncomfortable and unable to sleep at night. *How many mattresses would it take? How could a little pea bother her so?* At the beginning of every story, I marveled that, even with all of the cushioning, the mattresses never seemed to be enough to soothe the princess's discomfort. I was fascinated by all who came to help the princess find the key to her discomfort. In my young mind, I wondered, *Why is she so preoccupied with her rest, her beauty sleep?* I couldn't help but think, *Wasn't beauty found in makeup, in the lipstick that I longed to wear?*

I would always have a sense of anticipation and excitement when the storyteller, usually my mother or father, with perfect intonations of mystery, would report the finding of the pea in her bed. "And there under all of the mattresses was a dried-out, tiny little green pea," they would read. I always felt a sense of awe when the discovery was read to me. From my tomboy perspective, all I could think of at the end of every storytelling was, *How could a little pea make such a difference and cause so much distress? She must be a very sensitive princess!* Of course, you know the ending of the story. The pea was removed and the princess married the prince and hopefully, at least for a little while, slept soundly.

A Pebble in the Shoe

I like to compare the cumbersome pea to the limited belief that keeps you from getting the nurturing you need. The layers of mattresses are like your walls of self-protection. They work to a certain extent, but you know when "something isn't quite feeling right." You know when something is disturbing your efforts to get in balance with yourself. At this point, your task is to unearth the buried belief so you can find rest and get back on track with yourself. To do so, you will turn to the wall itself, which, as I've mentioned before, holds the clues to the mysteries within. To prepare you for how to approach the work that follows, I have a little story to share with you.

True Story

AT A CERTAIN point in his life, the famous psychiatrist Carl Jung was wondering what triggered the state of imagination. One day, still pondering the issue, he was standing on a platform in a train station in Zurich, Switzerland, waiting for his train. While waiting and musing, he glanced up to see the magnificent Alps. He began to wonder, *What is on the other side of the mountain? Who lives there?* He began to play. He made up little stories in his mind, when suddenly he realized he was using his imagination. The experience of play, as opposed to cognitive thought, sparked the very thing he was looking for! Excited, he began to ask other passengers on the platform what they thought might be on the other side of the mountain. Each one had a different take on the same question, which solidified the beginning of Jung's hypothesis about the nature of imagination.

Fairy Tales, Faith, and Flow

WHY NOT USE what works? Let's go back to our imaginary journey and, for the purpose of learning more about the guards at the gate, let's see how outrageous, creative, and playful we can be.

Our Story: Imagine...

WE ARE IN a very mellow mood. We have had a day of rest. We are sitting in shade with our backs leaning against a couple of tree trunks that flank the stream close to the B&B where we are spending the night. By now we have had several talks about what it means to preserve our feminine nature in a man's world. We find the topic of discussion interesting and have recently started to help each other see through the eyes of the feminine.

On this particular afternoon, we are contemplating how to dig deeper. We realize that if we are going to take ourselves seriously and put ourselves at the top of our priority list, we have to find a way into the realm of emotional vulnerability. *Why is taking care of ourselves so hard to sustain?* we wonder. We know we can do it now and again, but what about it all the time? We confess the issue is the reason why we are on the journey to begin with. We know we have to live differently, not reinvent ourselves, but the way we live in the world. We chuckle as, tongue in cheek, I share the thought, "Taking long treks to find ourselves could, after all, become an expensive habit!"

As we continue to talk lightly, I suggest we make up a fairy tale that represents our dilemma. "What the hell," we say together. "It's not like we have anything else going on right now." We set about creating a theme for the fairy tale, which we ultimately decide is to uncover the buried belief, the "secret key" that restricts us from taking care of ourselves with a heart full of trust and grace.

You start: "Let's imagine a sacred pool with mysterious restorative powers."

I pipe in. "Powers that set us free to become wise, beautiful, and whole."

You add, "The pool is enclosed in a secret garden behind a wall."

We both groan. "Yes, all around the wall are formidable guards who won't let us by."

We laugh as we add the names of the people we imagine holding us back from ourselves. Together, we turn our attention inward to separately consider the part of ourselves, the voice that is holding us back. Once fully settled, we contemplate all that the fairy tale implies to each one of us.

To be continued...

Perfectionism is the voice of the oppressor, the enemy of the people. It will keep you cramped and insane your whole life....

—

Anne Lamott

THE BEAUTY OF WRITING

14. Write Your Heart Out (Journal writing)
Theme: *Self-Awareness/Limiting Belief*

Like Jung, who was pondering how to engage the unconscious without putting a cognitive spin on it, you will imaginatively immerse yourself in the voice of your character strategy, the guard at the gate, to find the impact such a presence has on your life.

Although you have played before, play/imagine now with all your heart. Imagine, like we did in Our Story, what the guards at your inner gate might be yelling at you. What are the messages they hurl at you? What are the taunts that trigger obsessive worry, stop you dead in your tracks, and thus keep your inner woman from flourishing?

PREPARATION
- Take a long, deep breath. Center yourself in your body. Be aware of your posture.
- Bring to mind a time when you tried to nurture yourself, care for your needs, and got scared off because you felt vulnerable and/or guilty that your needs might disappoint or hurt someone else.

Imagine one of the prompts below to be the loud, intimidating voice of the guard. Choose the prompt that resonates most with you.

DON'T YOU KNOW THAT IF YOU...?
WHAT MAKES YOU THINK...?

Write for three minutes in your journal.

14a. Write Your Heart Out (cultivating resonance)
Theme: *Self-Awareness/Limiting Beliefs*

*Only the heart
knows how to find
what is precious.*

—

Fyodor Dostoyevsky

Let's deepen the experience of getting to know your inner voices by creating a mind/body connection with the work you have just completed.

Preparation

- Please read the work you have just completed aloud.
- As you read, notice which sentence, word, or message rings a bell with you and makes you shudder. Underline the sentence, word, or message that resonates with you the most.

Record what you have underlined on the line below.

_____

_____

_____

_____

Lavender Notes

Becoming sensitive to what is going on in your body is a fabulous tool that helps you flag and differentiate between when you are in the realm of your authentic core self and when you are not.

The longer you are disconnected from your true nature, the more stressed out you become. In the fairy tale of the "Princess and the Pea," the princess was bitchy for a reason! She needed her beauty rest and she knew it. When you get bitchy, it's a signal that you need to go in search of the pea—or, in this case, the limiting belief that hides in the wall of your character strategy.

14b. Write Your Heart Out (Mind-Body Observations)
Theme: *Physical Discernment*

Write down any physical observations you notice in your body as a result of reading your resonant sentence. For example, you may notice a caving in of your chest or a tightening in your stomach when you read the message from the guards.

_____

_____

_____

_____

Beauty Metaphor
Having great posture makes you feel fabulous.

Developing Mind-Body Support

Learning to observe your mind-body state is a skill that gives you the opportunity to shift out of a collapsed demeanor if a limiting belief is present. For example, if you notice when you read your resonant work that your chest caves in a little, then mindfully lengthen your spine and pull your shoulders back a bit without becoming rigid. Notice how from your new mind-body perspective you may feel less anxious. If your tummy is tight, breathe into the tightness. Stay with the process of observation, without trying to control the outcome, until the tightness subsides. Make sure you sit up straight during this process to literally give your stomach more breathing room. Play and explore. Be creative; ask your body what it might need to relieve any tension you may be feeling.

Lavender Notes

Reframing the daunting voice of the guard from an ominous presence into a nurturing presence takes time and practice, as well as discipline of spirit. Practice presence. As you progress, be loving and gentle with yourself. Take it easy. Learn and absorb at your own pace. From here until the end of the chapter, enjoy the upcoming mini psych-education information. The purpose is to help you set realistic expectations for the path ahead.

Wherever You Go, the Guards Go!

Circumventing the intellect to access the felt experience of the inner feminine is similar to outsmarting the guards that protect your inner wall. Undoubtedly, you are now fully aware of the cognitive internal arguments that keep you stuck in your head, in fear of self-actualization. Just as the guards in the fairy tale become menacing when you experientially, pick in hand, begin to dismantle the wall, so do the voices in your head become activated when you begin to make progress in your attempt to connect with your authentic self. As you might have guessed, the voices of the guards and the voices in your head are one and the same. They make up what is called your false self, the part of you that keeps you out of touch with your authentic core self.

Little Big Transition Bridge

As you experientially move beyond the default role of emotional caretaker into the realm of the authentic woman, you come into direct contact with your inner wall, also called your false self. The experience can leave you feeling disoriented. It is normal to feel ungrounded and a little confused when you work at the edge of your window of tolerance, which is the clinical way of saying "at the edge of your emotional comfort zone." For a short period, you may feel lost and the world may look fuzzy. You may wonder, *Who am I? Which part of me is real?*

The inner conflict becomes your moment of truth, where the past and the present momentarily come alive and are simultaneously held together in your heart. Your task is to have the courage to continue forward into the unknown to forge new beliefs about yourself. Like having a light face peel, crossing the bridge that links the old and the new may leave you temporarily feeling raw and naked without protection.

The Paradox of Change

At this point, there is only one question to answer: Are you going to listen to the voices in your head telling you to turn back because it's not safe, or are you going to stay steady, slow down, and learn a little more about where you find yourself each moment in time? To become familiar with where you are, it helps to be able to tolerate feelings of disorientation! Like new skin exposed to fresh air, you are may feel pings of vulnerability. When you can hold discomfort in your heart, like your flowers are contained in the vase, you allow yourself to be comforted with the knowledge that you are on the right path.

True Story

JANE WAS WORKING with the idea of letting herself be an emotional priority in her life. Together, we talked about what that would look like. Jane began to explore her inner barrier. "If I'm not going to pay attention to my own needs, how can I expect anyone else to?" she asked assuredly during a moment of deep insight. She paused before she continued to reflect. "It's just that if I really take responsibility for what I'm saying, things will have to change. What will my husband and children think? They won't be used to me thinking or acting like that!"

What is interesting about Jane's inquiry is that she was viewing her option to put herself first through the lens of others, instead of her own point of view. She was letting the guards at the gate intimidate her away from caring for herself. To help her correct her frame of reference, I gently said, "Jane, the real question is: How will *you* feel when you put others to the side, so you can nurture yourself?" With my comment, Jane realized that the frame of reference she had created disempowered her and that she needed to reframe her frame. She looked at me and smiled. "Okay, then, you caught me," she said playfully.

Redirected, she mindfully began to explore putting herself first. In doing so, she directed the focus of her inquiry away from others. She avoided being disenchanted and trapped by what others thought and felt about her choices.

Easier Said Than Done

IF YOU LOOK at where Jane is in her self-renewal journey, you know she is being challenged by the choice to stay open. She is facing herself and experiencing what it really means for her to be first. Some of the questions she is facing are: Can she tolerate the attention she is giving herself without believing she is selfish/unworthy? What is she letting go of? What is she deciding to reach for? Who is she becoming? How will she feel standing in the limelight of her life? Will she experientially be able to tolerate living in an expanded state of openness? What will happen to "the take-charge side of her" as she lives in faith, from the feminine experience?

Familiar with the challenges associated with the opening-up process, Jane is able to lovingly laugh at herself when she catches herself listening to the voice of her guard. With the skill to flag her experience, she is able to change direction. Armed with the frame of reference that she wants to champion her inner woman, she is able to redirect her focus and get back on course.

Please notice the importance of having the loving feminine as a frame of reference to orient toward.

Lavender Notes

As you journey inward, keep in mind our frame of reference, which is to reconnect with the woman within. Like a star guides sailors at night, let the feminine frame of reference support you as you open up within.

Explore the Gift

Every shift in awareness brings with it the gift of exploration. Each gift when explored awakens the guards at the gate. The greater the shift, the bigger the reaction of the guards; remember, they are not deaf! Any slight movement in the direction of the mysterious garden within puts them on high alert. Therefore, keeping the feminine experience in mind, the question becomes how to soften the hearts of the guards so they do not perceive you as a threat. What can you do to turn the guards, the voices linked to the past, into friends that allow you to come and go as you please in the garden of your heart? How will you integrate them into your present experience and let them know you still need the service of their protection, just not in the same way?

Beauty Metaphor

When you begin a rejuvenation regimen, you do not look in the mirror and expect to see immediate results. The idea is foolish. It takes time to bring the glow back into lifeless-looking skin.

In the same way, it takes time to actualize some of the ideas put forth in this book. You have to be willing to be patient, like Jane, and take it a step at a time. On the other hand, you do want to know what to look for and what to expect out of your efforts.

Let's create a frame of reference for the renewal work you are doing. Let's reframe any false notions you have about manifesting swift changes, and transform your notions into realistic expectations. The list of expectations below is specifically linked to the process of opening up and deconstructing the wall of your character strategy.

List of Expectations
1. Expect insights, not solutions to a problem.
2. Expect confusion, not clarity of purpose.
3. Expect moments of Aha! without doing anything about the experience.
4. Expect a little discomfort, not the ease of familiarity.
5. Expect to sense the direction ahead, not a well-laid-out map.

Embrace the Paradox of Becoming

Remember, you are on a journey of "becoming," which inherently implies you do not arrive. Please, enjoy the journey as it unfolds. Treasure the experiences you are having. Imagine them to be stepping stones leading you toward your authentic self.

A little lipstick, if you please!

There is nothing as appealing as a woman who feels vibrant and healthy from the inside out. When you look at her, the mystery of her essence captivates you. It is as if she knows some secret you don't know.

Inner Glamour Tips

Claim your light. Let the glamour within shine through. To access the beautiful presence of who you are, let's have you open up and practice what I call the Body Walk.

Read through all the instructions before implementing. Give yourself five minutes for this exercise.

I only like the color red on my roses, my lipstick and the bottom of my shoes.

—

Chanel Dudley

- To begin, stand up straight. Be supple in your stance, as opposed to rigid.
- Take a beautiful, deep breath. Notice if your head is tilted to the side or looking straight ahead.
- Feel your feet on the ground. Go barefoot for extra pleasure.
- Now quietly start walking. Just walk for a moment. Find a slow, mindful pace that suits your mood. For example, if you have been a wimp lately, you might want to walk a little faster, with purpose, to feel your power. If you are a take-charge woman, slow down. Feel your grace.
- Whatever you do, please do not collapse your chest, go weak-kneed, or let your arms go limp.
- To lengthen your spine, gently pull up your rib cage and expand to your full height.
- As you walk, drop your shoulders and keep your head held

high—not nose in the air. (Note: Please do not force your posture or stick your boobs out unless, of course, you usually hide "the girls." This key is to allow your body to find its own cadence and rhythm.)

- Now, as you walk gently, tell yourself: "I am free to be myself, the beautiful woman I am meant to be."
- Notice the sensations you feel when you utter these words.
- If you can, do the Body Walk for about fifteen to twenty minutes and notice what happens to your posture, your thoughts, and the attitude you have toward yourself.

Outer Glamour Tips

- Apply a little liner on the outside of your lip line.
- Slick on your lipstick with a little dab of gloss in the middle of the lower lip.

7

Sneaking In and Out of the Garden of the Unconscious

SNEAKING IS ABOUT getting what you want and or need unseen, which is what this short little chapter is all about. Sneaking is also about having the belief that you would not be given or get what you desire if you asked directly—which, when it comes to expecting support from the part of you mired in limiting beliefs, is definitely true. Therefore, it pays to be clever and sneaky when you seek access into the garden of the authentic feminine, especially when the purpose is to begin the process of dismantling the inner wall in order to set the inner woman free.

Don't you know that "No" is the wildest word we consign to language?
—
Emily Dickinson

Short and Sweet *(author's story)*

One can never consent to creep when one feels an impulse to soar.

—

Helen Keller

THRILL SEEKERS. I can remember the night I trespassed onto forbidden waterfront property to go swimming under cover of a dark, black night with a group of friends.

The Secret in the Mysterious Clues

WHAT HAPPENS WHEN you learn that the property you thought you were sneaking onto belongs to you? Suddenly, you feel foolish—like, what is the point of hiding? The exposure brings with it a silver lining, an awakening into a consciousness. From your expanded place of awareness you wonder, *How come I didn't know the beautiful property belonged to me?* Fueled by curiosity and desire, you start to investigate. Your investigation connects you to the land and draws you in further.

Therapeutically speaking, the same thing is true of the mysterious garden within, the one your free-spirited little girl walked away from so long ago. Let's use what you know, to find answers to the question, *What would lead a child to disconnect from her authentic, loving self?* From the point of view of your character strategy, you might begin the process by asking yourself, "What would lead a child to believe she had to be cute, manipulative, or indirect in order to be heard, accepted? What would compel a child to believe it wasn't okay to shine, that it was up to her to make her parent happy? What would lead a child to believe there was no one around, that to find support she had to turn to herself?" And, most important, "Why would any child feel it was not okay to be authentically, emotionally dependent?"

Finally, "What is the embedded message in the limited belief that tells your little girl it is not okay to be herself?" To find the limited belief that lies at the core of the original rupture, let's continue to explore the essence of your character strategy.

THE BEAUTY OF WRITING

Identify Your Character Strategy (Wall)

The purpose of the following writing experience is to give voice to the ulterior motives embedded in each strategy. To keep your exploration fresh and thus maintain a state of curiosity, which naturally triggers the brain into a seeking mode, I compared each character strategy (wall) to a plant, flower, or tree. As such, play along as you imagine a world where plants, flowers, or trees talk and reveal to you the secrets of their forbidden mysteries. Remember, exploration is what matters here! All you have to do is participate and follow along.

PREPARATION

Enjoy the guided meditation to open your mind.

- Please use your breath to get aligned and centered in your body.
- To support the imaginative state, soften your gaze. Literally pull the energy and intensity in your gaze to the backs of your eyes.
- Allow yourself to drift into a realm of make believe where the imaginative comes alive and makes sense of the illogical.

Now, read through the list of plants/flowers/trees below:

- Morning Glory
- Sweet Thorny Rose
- Sycamore Suffocated by Mistletoe
- Cactus

Dreams are illustrations… from the book your soul is writing about you.

—

Marsha Norman

Contemplate the characteristics of each flower, plant, or tree listed above. Ask yourself: What would make each plant, flower, and/or tree a desirable choice for a barrier? For example, a cactus has visible thorns, which sends the message, "Stay away." The sycamore suffocated by mistletoe can't breathe, be seen, or feel her beauty.

15. Write Your Heart Out

Theme: *Insight/Awareness of Voice of False Self*

Continue to maintain a state of play; complete each prompt below to find the one you resonate with right now. Write from the first person—i.e., as if you were the Morning Glory. Use your senses to open up the experience. Write uncensored. Write fast. Have fun.

Morning Glory:
Ms. Busyness! State of mind: Perfectionist
I cover as much ground as I can so _____

_____

Because if I don't, _____

_____

My biggest worry is _____

_____

Fragrant Thorny Rose:
Ms. Compliant! State of Mind: Pleaser
I attract you with my fragrant scent so_____

_____

Because, if I don't, _____

_____

My biggest worry is _____

_____

Sycamore Suffocated by Mistletoe:

Ms. Yeah-But! State of Mind: Martyr

I give you my sunshine so _____

_____

Because if I don't, _____

_____

My biggest worry is _____

_____

Cactus: Ms. I Can Do It Myself!

State of Mind: Isolationist

I'm low maintenance so _____

_____

Because if I'm not _____

_____

My biggest worry is _____

_____

*Most of the sighs
we hear have
been edited.*

—

Stanislaw Jerzy Lec

Lavender Notes

When I conduct workshops, I have the women in the group read and share their writing out loud. The purpose of this activity is to have each woman experience the sound of her voice, the story of her upset, while receiving support. When you read your work out loud, it is often common to hear a message you might have missed when you were writing. I would like you to have a similar experience.

15a. Write Your Heart Out (cultivating resonance)
Theme: *Insight/Awareness of Voice of False Self*

PREPARATION
- Take a deep breath. Center yourself.
- Mentally prepare to connect with your voice.
- As you read out loud, please read very slowly so you create a mind-body connection.
- Become aware of your voice connecting with the words you are reading.
- If you receive any insights, do not pick them apart or use them to beat yourself up. Just notice what you see and hear.

To continue the process of creating an ongoing writing program to be used at the end of our journey, please make sure to take a moment to identify and underline the words or sentence that you resonate with the most. Out of all of the categories, only select one resonant sentence.

Record your resonant word(s) or sentence below.

FYI: Please note the description of plant, flower, or tree in which you discovered your resonant sentence. This would be the character strategy you identify with the most at this moment in time.

_____

_____

I find it interesting to hear what others think and feel. I find listening to the different perspectives nurturing. With that idea in mind, I thought you might like to see what other women have written from the point of view of their strategy. So without further ado, let's put on some gardening shoes and get back out among the plants.

Case Studies: Finding the Story in the Story

Here are some stories written by women who engaged in the process you just completed.

One woman wrote from the point of view of a Morning Glory:

I know I'm hearty. I crawl up fences and make them look pretty. I like to be useful so I look for places to fill up. "Look and see how I can grow all over the place." I'm always in a hurry. There is so much growing to do. I want to make my mistress happy so I grow really, really fast. I never stop and rest. I keep going because if I don't you won't find me useful and productive. Then what will happen to me?

The main issue here: avoidance of stillness. Fear of what might happen without a productive purpose.

Written from the point of view of the Fragrant Thorny Rose:

I'm coy. I come alive when you notice me. I will do anything to please you, to get you to look my way. I will use my sweet fragrance to dazzle you; it gets you every time. I will sing and dance to any tune you wish, to keep you interested and close to me. My secret desire is for you to tell me I'm the prettiest, most special rose in the whole garden. I will mesmerize you with tales. I will twist and turn every which way, because if I don't, you will see my thorns and you might look at me disapprovingly, or go away.

The main issue here: the avoidance of being direct. Fear of what might happen if you express needs in a straightforward way!

Written from the point of view of a Sycamore Suffocated by Mistletoe:

Okay, climb all over me. Take away my sunshine. Hang on me to the point of hiding me. I can endure it! You seem to need the light more than me anyway. Sigh. The thing is, the more I give, the more you take. I can barely breathe. The situation is hopeless. I want to get you off my back, disentangle myself from you; yet I let you stay because if I don't you'll tighten your squeeze and suffocate me with your anger. Besides, how would you live without me?

The main issue here: fear of anger as well as the avoidance of feeling entitled to have fun and shine.

Written from the point of view of a Cactus:

I'm tough. I'm strong. I can take the heat. All I need is a little water to thrive. In case you haven't noticed, I display my thorns right up front, out in the open. Hopefully you'll get the message and "Stay Away. Leave Me Alone." On occasion I do sport a beautiful flower that sits on the top of my head like a fascinator, the way the English girls do. To notice the bright colors in my hat, you have to be in the right place at the right time. I save my flower for special occasions because if I don't I'll draw attention to the one thing I cherish most: the way I can be tender and sweet in spite of my intense nature.

The main issue here: inability to lean, fear of vulnerability, and denial of the need to have needs.

Beauty Metaphor

After corrective surgery for drooping eyelids, you are instructed not to fuss with your eyes. To avoid scarring and facilitate healing, you are asked to rest and avoid strenuous exercise! You expect to feel discomfort and to look like a mess. On the other side of the ordeal, you will not only see better, you will look and feel prettier.

True Story

There is a point in therapy when the person I am working with has the brilliant idea to get rid of the part of her that she perceives as causing a problem. "Can you help me cut out this part of myself?" is the universal plea I often hear. "I can help you learn to open up to your feelings and learn to live with your feelings in a way that will help you flourish, but I can't help you cut them out. Your feelings are a part of you!" This is the only honest answer I have to give.

Hold back twitchy fingers!

You have just completed some very significant work. You have peeled back layers of your defense strategy. At this juncture, please avoid the temptation to pick at yourself or try and fix a problem you may have discovered. Both are common tendencies to try to get back in control. Instead, focus on creating space in your heart to hold with love and compassion the work you are doing. As you do so, be aware of the new ideas and feelings that fill up the space inside of you.

A little lipstick, if you please!

Inner Glamour Tips
- Let your inner lady lounge. Take a big stretch; let out a yawn. Do this a few times.
- Have a wonderful cup of hot tea.
- For strength have a few almonds.
- Go out for a short, meandering walk.
- Experience sensuality. Breathe in and enjoy the fragrance of a beautiful flower.
- Refresh the flowers in your special vase to remind yourself that your feelings matter and that you deserve to take up space.

Outer Glamour Tips
- Admire yourself.
- Take a nice, long look at yourself in the mirror.
- Notice some special feature you love about your lips!
- If you don't notice anything special, then, all the more, try a new lipstick.
- Special little tip: If your teeth have a yellow tint to them, stay away from orange lipsticks! They don't help. Go for more of a red.

A woman who doesn't wear lipstick feels undressed in public. Unless she works on a farm.

—

Unknown

8

Going Deep

T O EXPERIENCE EXPERIENCES, it is important to get out of your head and have life experiences, not just think about them. For example, to feel safe and agile in water, it helps to know how to swim in the deep end. To navigate the nuances of the deep, you learn how to float and flow, as well as hold your breath if needed. To experience freedom in the water, you follow the water safety rules. To expand your capacity to play, you continually hone your skills as a swimmer.

Ultimately, you build respect for the waters you swim in, whether it is a pool, river, lake, or ocean. Becoming a master swimmer, however, requires a new level of commitment. The moment requires you to really make a decision to either get into or out of the water, so to speak.

In the same way, there is a transition moment in the therapeutic process that requires you to move beyond the talking phase of therapy. To progress, you need the courage to put your heart on the line by risking feelings of vulnerability. The very

We do not learn by experience, but by our capacity for experience.

—

Buddha

action of experiencing your vulnerability in the presence of a caring other is what helps you access the deepest part of yourself. To swim in the waters of your soul, you let go and flow with the experiential shifts taking place within you as you open up.

In this chapter, you will expand into the authentic feeling part of the opening-up process you are engaged in. At first, the experience of change may feel difficult. However, just as it is when you learn to swim in deep water, you make a decision to trust and practice faith, in the hope that everything you have learned so far will hold you up and keep you afloat.

Moment of Truth

IN THERAPY, WHEN a person starts to open up and trust, they feel anxious. They feel like they are losing control. When this natural phenomenon occurs, which paradoxically signifies progress, it is common for clients to critically question the purpose of their therapy. Often, the client will secretly blame the therapist for unearthing feelings they do not want to face and acknowledge.

The moment is fragile, yet it is the moment you wait for because it is filled with authentic possibility. Through the experience of confronting and openly expressing their feelings of disconnect with the therapist, a client is able to repair the inner discord while remaining in relationship. To bring about conflict resolution, you stay connected to the experience of conflict so you can work through the nuances of conflict to each other's satisfaction. You are going to apply the principles of conflict resolution to your blind spot, to help you transcend the deep-seated conflict between your false self, the part of you associated with your character strategy, and your authentic self, specifically your inner woman.

FYI: If your journey has been successful, then about now you might be experiencing two separate worlds coexisting within you: the world of the false self (associated with the guards) and the world of the authentic self, which for our purposes is associated with feminine presence.

As a result of the schism, you undoubtedly feel tension triggered by the duality of your inner experience. If you feel, or have ever felt, an actual tug of war happening within you, usually in your abdomen, then you know the place I'm talking about.

Paradox of Openness

THE TRUTH IS that during the overall opening-up process, it is common to feel yourself shutting down as you are simultaneously opening up. While a part of you may be yelling, "No, no more! I can't go there," another part of you may be saying, "Go for it." This is all part of the expansion process. Compare the transition to the moment a swimmer gets ready to jump off the high diving board for the first time. You can imagine the swimmer wondering if she has made a mistake taking her experience so far. Before she dives, she may look at her coach with a look that says, "Make sure you have my back." My answer to you is, "Yes, I do."

A Wink

A LITTLE EMBEDDED treasure has been intentionally inserted into your program to bring you to a place of therapeutic discomfort. Yes, I know it doesn't seem very nice of me. However, my intent is to guide you into feeling enough discomfort that you will then be motivated to let go and shift out of your patterns of disconnect. Otherwise, the process of rupture and the dynamic of relationship disengagement continue. There is another truth, which is: I don't want this book to be another self-help book you read and then put back on the shelf. I sincerely want to facilitate change so that your inner woman is set free to come out, dance in the world, and fiercely sing her song for all to hear.

In my story, which comes next, I share with you a seemingly easy moment to transition through, which for me became a huge challenge and major crossroads in my life. The story is about a moment where I consciously made the choice to open up and experience discomfort, in order to create a growth opportunity for myself. I like to compare the experience to standing on the edge of the high diving board and taking the dive.

My Sunrise at Campobello *(author's story)*

"LIFE HAS RHYTHM. Growth has its own flow. Let the mystery unfold and go with the flow." These were the words rolling around in my head as I sat amidst a group of women in a lovely living room overlooking the Saint Lawrence Seaway. Beyond my wildest dreams, there I was spending the weekend in the summer retreat home that once belonged to Eleanor and Franklin Roosevelt. I couldn't believe the synchronicity of the event. I had just been contemplating some of Eleanor's quotes on women and strength when the call came from my cousin Kathleen. She was inviting me to a small gathering of women she was putting together to share ideas. As a woman who leads retreats, I jumped at the idea of participating in one. Besides, I rationalized that it would be downright crazy to say no to spending time on Eleanor's private stomping grounds of Campobello!

So there I was, sitting in the wonderful rambling house, with great views in every direction, discussing women's issues, when I felt another ping. *You are here for a reason, to learn…*I told myself.

Just at that moment, Anisa, the self-appointed leader of what was supposed to be a leaderless group, said to me, "That's not what we are here for."

As it turned out, Anisa would not allow me to comment on much of anything, especially when I aimed my therapeutic (caretaking) insights toward the woman who was speaking. *Who died and appointed you leader? Blah-blah-blah* was the self-talk in my head. Yet, another part of me was curious. She had my attention. Anisa's words, a force of nature, carried with them a piercing chill. So I sat still. Instead of giving in to my defensive reaction, which would have been to explain what I was doing, or politely call her on "her issue," which was to interject her opinion, I decided to accept Anisa's comments, be quiet, and see what I could learn.

The truth is that Anisa's ability to stand up to my default caretaking behavior redirected me toward a new way of being and belonging in the group. I realized that Anisa's control issues mirrored mine and thus became, through a willingness to see myself in a less than favorable light, a gift in disguise. My willingness to let Anisa's "No" have value left me stripped bare and feeling emotionally vulnerable, naked. Surrendered, I sat and learned through raw experience what it meant to just be. I learned that my voice did not have to always contribute "help." I could just be myself and crack the joke that authentically welled up in me every now and then. I found out how closely intertwined my character strategy was with the authentic woman. I could actually feel how they were both wrapped up inside of me, like branches of a ficus tree that over time had become enmeshed, fused into one trunk. Unless you looked closely, you could not tell the two branches, the two parts of me, apart.

Dance of the Double Bind: Now You See Me and Now You Don't!

THE DISCOVERY OF your character strategy is often felt as ephemeral, both enticing and formidable. The double bind offers an opening that can bring doubt and guilt as well as the excitement of exploring more. You feel led to go beyond your inner system of protection at the very same time that your character strategy is pulling out all the stops to hold you back and to keep you safe. The key is to decide which message you are going to listen to. Are you going to listen to the cry of the false self, the voice of the guards at the barrier that promise security? Or are you going to heed the unfamiliar call of the sensuous feminine, the authentic self who whispers quietly, yet insistently, that she holds the key to your heart, your happiness?

By having the courage and commitment to identify, and thus name, your character strategy, you open up your awareness process. You take the first step required to dismantle your inner barrier. In the process, you get an inkling of the story that tells of the forgotten needs of the child, your younger self that was left behind after the rupture.

With each step of your journey you make a conscious decision to move forward. Before and after each exercise you created a mind-body connection. You have also given voice and legitimacy to the deepest part of yourself by identifying and then recording your resonant words.

Acknowledge Expansion

I'D SAY IT'S time to acknowledge the emotional stamina you are developing. Imagine! Take a moment to realize how many aspects of yourself you are learning to hold all at once. You are containing many different thoughts, sensations, and feelings simultaneously. You have moved beyond pure cognitive thought! You are actively expanding within. When you have the strength to hold a space within that allows you to let go of what you need to leave behind, while at the same time opening up to what is coming in, you are truly living in the land of the sacred! I like to compare the experience of openness to living in the palm of the hand of the universal feminine where you can be yourself, feel safe, and know that all is possible.

There are only hints and guesses, hints followed by guesses, and the rest is prayer, observance, discipline, thought, and action.

—

T. S. Eliot

THE BEAUTY OF WRITING

16. Write Your Heart Out
Theme: *Assessment Current Strategy*

Awareness is change. Let's facilitate your opening-up process by exploring more closely the nuances and liabilities of each character strategy. The idea is to become familiar with the telltale signs of the hidden conflict and behaviors associated with each strategy so you can flag them. You may want to think of it as a ranger putting out flags around areas of thin ice. When you see the flags, you consciously choose to walk in a different direction to avoid mishap.

The questions on the next page represent aspects of the mind-set of each character strategy. The mind-set represents the lens through which each character strategy views the world, the lens that needs repair.

PREPARATION
- As always, please take a breath to get centered.
- Read each question carefully and go with your gut response to answer the question.
- Please answer the questions in all of the strategies to discover which strategy you lean on.
- To gain the full benefit of the exercise, be earnest in your effort to answer the questions.

For the Go-Getter Character Strategy: (Morning Glory)

Yes No (*Please check one or the other.*)

1. __ __ Do you ever wonder why people look to you for information?
2. __ __ Do you ever wish others would plan the activity you want to do?
3. __ __ Do you sometimes feel like you don't exist if you are not working hard?
4. __ __ Do you wish you could turn off your mind or get it to stop racing?
5. __ __ Do you feel like there is always more you could do?

For the Sweet Talker Character Strategy: (Fragrant Thorny Rose)

Yes No (*Please check one or the other.*)

1. __ __ Do you often wish you would be taken seriously?
2. __ __ Do you feel like you are not good enough?
3. __ __ Do you feel invisible?
4. __ __ Do you often say yes and then later wish you'd said no?
5. __ __ Do you wish you could tell someone off and then don't?

For the Grin and Bear It Character Strategy: (Sycamore Suffocated by Mistletoe)

Yes No (*Please check one or the other.*)

1. __ __ Do you wonder about just how insensitive others can be?
2. __ __ Do you feel underappreciated for all that you give?
3. __ __ Do you feel like you endure life rather than enjoy life?
4. __ __ Do you feel a constant, low-level irritation burning inside of you?
5. __ __ Do you look at the world through the lens of a glass half full?

For the Self-Reliant Character Strategy: (Cactus)

Yes No (*Please check one or the other.*)

1. __ __ Do you dislike hearing how strong you are?
2. __ __ Do you turn inward when you feel upset?
3. __ __ Do you have difficulty trusting and feeling safe in the hands of others?
4. __ __ Do you prefer to work on a task alone?
5. __ __ Do you feel uncomfortable asking others for a favor?

16a. Write Your Heart Out

Theme: *Assessment Current Strategy*

PREPARATION

- Please center yourself with your breath.
- Add up all of the yeses and the noes in each strategy. Notice which strategy has the most yeses. This is your strategy, which you will record in the space below. It doesn't matter if it is different from one you identified with before. Remember, you are building awareness. You don't have to live in the land of black-and-white answers.

FYI: If you end up with a similar number of yeses in more than one character strategy, then go to question number three. See in which strategy you checked off the word *yes*. If you checked off *yes* for both answers, then pick the question you resonate with the most. The category your *yes* answer falls under will be your identified character strategy.

Please fill in your answer:

Currently, the character strategy I identify with the most is:

_____

In the strategy you selected, notice the issue you identified with the most and record it below.

_____

A secondary strategy I identify with is (if there is one):

_____

In the strategy you selected, notice the issue you identified with the most and record it below.

_____

Customize Your Work

Going forward, the areas you identified are perfect focal points—issues to flag. Seeing the flagged behavior(s) reminds you to be conscious. The flags also remind you that in the present moment, like I did with Anisa, you have the opportunity to take contrary action so you can keep moving in the direction of openness. Now, is that cool or what? With the information at your fingertips, you can actually create a map for your self-renewal journey based on the areas that need specific repair.

Clues in Your Background Story

Know the issues around which each barrier is built. I'm sure you also notice that many issues appear similar and seem replicated in each strategy. In many ways, you are right. The truth is, most children like to be productive, want to be liked, want to play and have fun, as well as feel a sense of autonomy while feeling secure. Each desire represents a stage in the early childhood developmental process. Depending upon what was occurring in your household, you may not have received the recognition or support you needed to successfully complete the developmental stage you were in; hence, the barrier. To thrive, you found ways to compensate for what you did not get when you were your authentic self.

Every Family Has a Story

Possibly, when you were young, your family ran into financial issues or was concerned with status and "making it;" thus, your need to be productive. Others of you may have a mother who was not really the nurturing type and thus the impulse or competition with a sibling to win favor and recognition by being cute or smart. Others may have had a mother who did not get enough mothering and who looked to you for what she did not get. Unaware, she took away your sparkle and you took on the burden of her neglect. In a similar fashion, I have known some women who have famous mothers and felt invisible around them because, through no doing of their own, the mothers received a lot of admiration and attention. Depending upon your family history, you chose a strategy most acceptable to help you fit in to get what you needed; hence, the distortion of your authentic self.

Lavender Notes

All character strategies act as a cover, a mask to hide authentic dependency needs that went unmet in the eyes and experience of the child within. The unconscious act of self-protection, in childhood, is the beginning of what is called 'false self' and is the precursor to the development of a character strategy.

I did not lose myself all at once. I rubbed out my face over the years washing away my pain, the same way carvings on stone are worn down by water.

—

Amy Tan

17. Write Your Heart Out
Theme: *Identification Blind Spot*

Keeping in mind the frame of reference of authentically owning your needs, let's go straight into your heart of hearts to find out what unconsciously motivates you into manipulating those around you to get your needs met.

PREPARATION
- Take a long, deep breath.
- To center your work, let's stabilize the energy in your body before you answer the upcoming questions. To start, notice where in your body you are holding your energy. Are you holding it out in front of you? Is it toward your back? Is it in your stomach? Is it in your head? Are you holding your breath and thus feel no field of energy in your body?

- Once you locate your field of energy, focus on bringing it to the center of your body. You can do this by literally focusing on the energy. Then, like you use a mouse/pointer to drag information from one location to another location on your computer screen, use your mind's eye to direct your energy toward the center of your body.
- At all times, keep your feet firmly planted on the ground.
- Use your breath to solidify the experience.
- When you feel ready, complete the questions below. The intent behind each question is to teach you about the motivation of your false self and thus clarify why your current approach to taking care of yourself might not work. Good luck.

Please check off Yes or No below. Note how closely your caring for others is motivated by the need to care for yourself.

1. Do you secretly put someone else's needs at the top of your priority list because you hope that, if you care for their needs, they will then turn around and care for you when you need it?
    __ Yes __ No

2. Do you put someone else's needs at the top of your priority list because you fear that, if you don't, they will get angry or be disappointed with you?
    ___ Yes __ No

3. Do you put someone else's needs at the top of your priority list because you want to keep peace in the relationship?
    ___ Yes ___ No

4. Do you put someone else's needs at the top of your priority list because you believe you are selfish if you put yourself first?
    ___ Yes ___ No

5. Do you put someone else's needs at the top of your priority list because you feel angry or sad when you think about taking responsibility for your needs?
    ___ Yes ___ No

6. Do you put someone else's needs at the top of your priority list because you think it is unladylike or unromantic to put yourself at the top of your priority list?
    ___Yes ___No

7. Do you put someone else's needs at the top of your priority list because you never thought about being high on your own priority list?
    ___Yes ___No

8. Do you go numb when you think of a priority list, or don't relate to the idea of having emotional needs?
    ___Yes ___No

In reviewing your answers, can you see how you unconsciously try to get others to meet your needs without your directly taking responsibility for meeting your own needs?

18. **Write Your Heart Out**
     Theme: *Identification Need*

     Circle the need that motivates you. To create depth of awareness, bring your inner child into the process and see what she seeks.

     Love   Approval   Recognition   Peace   Safety   Self-Worth

Finding the Missing Piece

Let's link your relationship strategy to the limited belief you carry within. For example:

- **The Perfectionist, Go-Getter,** believes if she works hard she will get the approval she seeks.
- **The Pleaser, Sweet Talker,** believes if she is compliant she will get the recognition she seeks.
- **The Martyr, Grin and Bear It,** believes if she avoids conflict she will get the self-worth she seeks.
- **The Isolationist, Self-Reliant,** believes if she is self-sufficient she will find the safety she seeks.

Through the Lens of False Hope

Each strategy looks at the world from a point of view that incorporates actions that each person believes must be performed to get the desired love, attention, and safety necessary to function in the world, as opposed to knowing you can receive love, attention, and safety just by being your authentic self. From early on you learn to trust in the efficacy of your relationship strategy to get your needs met more than you trust your authentic self; hence, the hidden barrier.

19. Write Your Heart Out (Journal Writing)
Theme: *Exploration/Decision/Insight*

So that you have a moment to catch up with yourself and integrate the shifts within, please take time to do the exercise below so you may bring to the surface any insights percolating in your unconscious awareness as a result of the work you have done.

In every adult there lurks a child, an eternal child, something that is always becoming, is never completed, and calls for unceasing care, attention, and education.

—

C. G. Jung

*Leave tracks.
Just as others have
been way-pavers
for your good
fortune, so you
should aid those
who will follow
in your way.*

—

**the Honorable Ruth
Bader Ginsburg**

PREPARATION

- Take a nice, long, soothing breath. Center yourself.
- Pause. Open your heart. Take a moment to notice what disappointments you might need to let go of in order to make the possibility of putting yourself first a reality.

Write from the prompt below. Be fluid. Do not edit or look back. Be surprised by what emerges!

Prompt: Coming upon a fork in the road, she decided to take the path less traveled. As she did, she knew…

Write in your journal for three minutes.

19a. Write Your Heart Out (cultivating resonance)
Theme: *Exploration/Decision/Insight*

As you have before, let's solidify your experience and create a prompt for your on-going self-care practice.

PREPARATION

- Take a moment to connect with your breath.
- As you read what you have written, consciously connect with your voice.
- Notice and underline the sentence, word, or message that resonates with you.

Record your resonant message or inspiration in the space below.

_____

_____

_____

Living in the Picture of Your Life

You have come to the point in your journey where you are very aware both cognitively and experientially of your inner barrier, your character strategy. You have seen the guards and made it to the wall. You have glimpsed into the mysterious, the inner feminine, garden of your soul. For now, take a break. Practice some of the restorative suggestions below. The tips will connect you with your sensuality, and thus help you remain open to the woman within as you go about your day.

A little lipstick, if you please!

Sometimes, seeing what you do to yourself can become the motivation to change. I know that what I am going to suggest to you may seem awful. Yet please do the experiment as suggested, because it is so powerful and will motivate you to keep yourself whole and intact.

Inner Glamour Tips
Please read through instructions before implementing them.

- Go the florist and buy two roses, or use any other two flowers or plants with petals.
- Bring them home and with reverence put them side by side in a vase full of water.
- Notice how beautiful the roses are in their natural state. Imagine that each flower represents you!
- Decide which rose is going to represent the part of you that is whole and which rose is going to represent the part of you that you sabotage. For impact, I would encourage you to use the rose that is the most beautiful to be the one you use to pick apart.
- Quietly hold it for a moment. Look at the beauty of the rose intact.

Adding sound to movies would be like putting lipstick on Venus de Milo.

—

Mary Pickford

Read the list of prompts below. *Select and circle the words that resonate with you the most.*

√ **I can't exist and find peace of heart unless I am productive and work for it.**

√ **I am not worthy of love and recognition unless I am perfect.**

√ **I don't deserve to take up space and shine.**

√ **I can't trust anyone to have my back.**

Now comes the hard part.
- Very slowly, say out loud the sentence that resonates with you. As you do so, pull off one of the petals of the rose you chose to represent the part of you that you sabotage.
- Keep the petal as a reminder of how you hurt yourself.
- Repeat four times. Then put the rose back in the vase as a reminder to love yourself.
- Every time you feel tempted to rip yourself apart, let yourself know that the consequence of your behavior is that you will have to tear off another petal.

True Story

When I have done this experiment in workshops, the women have a very hard time with the exercise. Usually you hear exclamations like, "Oh, I don't want to do this! It hurts to do this! Oh, the poor rose!" In the end, the visual is strong and becomes the teacher when you see a group of beautiful women standing around the room with limp, barren rose stems in hand. Imagine this is what you do to your most authentic self and then you wonder why you feel depleted and lackluster.

Women have reported back to me that the image of the rose shorn of her petals is quite a deterrent when you are in a self-sabotaging mood. The good news is you now have enough awareness to make a choice that nurtures you.

Outer Glamour Tips

- Go through your makeup bag and get rid of all of your outdated or dried-up tubes of lipstick.
- Start over with a new lipstick.

9

Breaking In New Shoes

WOMEN LOVE SHOES. Interestingly enough, shoes, like your character strategy, create a mood and make you feel and look at the world in a certain way. Sadly, when you live from the default position of a professional caretaker, you are, metaphorically speaking, likely to have a wardrobe full of nursing shoes instead of sassy, sexy heels. And you wonder why you are not seen for the beautiful, sensuous woman you are! I say it's time to clear the closet of the old worn-out shoes (attitudes) you habitually wear to every occasion and bring in some new ones. Let's expand your emotional wardrobe so that your inner woman is tempted to come out and play, knowing she will be felt by you and seen by others in all her glory. I hope you notice: the key is not to get rid of your nursing shoes, but to go shopping!

As every woman knows, it is rare to buy a new pair of shoes without having to break them in. To get through the waiting period as your feet scream for the old soles, you dig deep within to keep yourself from slipping your feet back into what is comfy

To choose clothes, either in a store or at home, is to define and describe ourselves.

—

Alison Lurie

and familiar. You actually let yourself experience the feelings of being torn between what you know is comfortable and the new, irritating experience of discomfort, believing all will turn out well in the end. During the process, pain and excitement are experienced side by side. To get through each aching step, you hold in your mind's eye the excitement of what is to come while feeling your sore feet.

You are able to do this without much thought because ultimately, you view the complete experience through the lens of how fabulous you will look and feel once you are at ease in your new pair of shoes. The focus of your belief is what carries you through the process and makes it all worthwhile.

Let's see how the process relates to where you find yourself currently.

Shifting Beliefs

WHEN YOU OPEN up and shift perspective, you commonly experience the old beliefs and the new possibilities side by side. With each choice you make to leave the old ways behind, you empower the authentic woman within. You risk emotional vulnerability to expand. With each step you take, you shift your focus to incorporate a new way of being. I'm fairly certain at this point, because of all of the progress you have made, you feel a little rift inside. To help you gain ground in your journey, you are now going to take advantage of the rift. Tweak it a little. Like breaking in a new pair of shoes, you may feel a pinch of pain, which is temporary.

Lavender Notes

For those of you going through a hard time, I decided to share stories in this chapter that are poignant. The purpose is so you do not feel alone or think you are going crazy during moments of extreme discomfort. You are just in the midst of a difficult transition. The intent behind the stories is to transport you through the gauntlet of transition rather than talk about how to do it.

Walking the Path *(author's story)*

I SAW THE shadows of pain in my friend's eyes the moment she stepped out of her car. Standing at the head of the beautiful little dirt path that lines one of the canals in the Marina, I waited. She didn't need to say much; we were old friends. I knew the walk would be "one of those walks." My best friend had always wanted to be a mother. I knew this from the time we were teenagers. She was now in her mid-forties and was looking into adoption with her husband. She had already had one devastating experience when the mother of a child she was supposed to get changed her mind at the last minute.

On this particular day, my friend said, "We got a call from the lawyer." I said nothing. When she said nothing, I asked, "What did he have to say?" Holding her breath and barely able to get the words out, she said, "I haven't called him back. I don't think I can do this anymore. It's just too painful." Tears rolled down her cheeks. I knew my friend needed space. What can you say when someone who has gone through so much disappointment tells you that it's over? It was not the time for encouragement. It was a moment to honor the space my friend found herself in! I waited. We walked mostly in silence.

Sensing it was okay to speak, I ventured, "Well, how about giving the lawyer a call. Miracles do happen." "I'm too scared to," was all she could say. Knowing the eye of the grief storm was passing, I decided to push a little. "Well, I think it's worth a shot; you never know. You have come this far. We still have to believe that it's possible, even though I know you are wondering." We walked side by side, my friend holding the pain associated with the belief it was not meant to be and me on the other hand believing in hope. The two voices, experiences, coexisted. One

You gain strength, courage and confidence by every experience in which you really stop to look fear in the face.

—

Eleanor Roosevelt

did not nullify the other. There was no analyzing—just walking, talking, and listening. I knew one belief would win out over the other.

So, before we parted ways, I asked my friend to say a prayer, call the lawyer, and try again. Later that afternoon the phone rang. It was my friend: "He has a young woman who is actually looking for older parents," she whispered to me in a choked-up voice. After a few months, I became godmother to a beautiful little girl.

Awareness Is Key

As IT IS with any transition, there is a significant moment in the process of change when you are caught and torn between two worlds that simultaneously coexist in your psyche. One world holds the idea of turning back, while the other world calls you forth toward the new. Then, like ships passing in the night, one course takes hold and becomes dominant. If you let yourself be tempted by the siren of the past, you retreat and find yourself in a state of chronic anxiety, which is only relieved when you revisit your decision and choose to reach for your future. In either case, when you heed the call to open up and move forward, pain starts to fade, and a horizon of hope opens up before you. Then, depending upon the circumstance, the experience becomes a distant memory. You can imagine if the story of my friend had a different outcome; moving forward would entail going through a difficult grief process that would need to be dealt with and integrated for renewed hope to be possible.

One Breath, One Step at a Time

As YOU GET ready to step into the unknown, through another "Our Story," let's fortify your newfound awareness of the pitfalls that lay embedded in the mind-set of each character strategy. Remember, you are learning to see how you see from the perspective of your strategy, so you can shift out of the strategy with greater ease. Compare what you are about to do with visiting the old homestead one more time before you get ready to leave the home of your past.

Lavender Notes

To work at the edge of the window of tolerance, the edge of your emotional comfort zone, it helps to feel safe and secure and yet stimulated. Otherwise, you won't be able to really explore.

Our Story: Imagine...

WE HAVE BEEN hiking quite a bit. Our legs are getting strong and solid. Our stamina is increasing. At this moment, we find ourselves on top of a steep hill that took a lot of effort to climb. We are sitting there enjoying the beautiful view that surrounds us. The guide is getting ready to give us some instructions on how to walk down the backside of the hill. Apparently, the path we are to take is full of rocks, loose dirt, and stones. Not a good combination, for safety reasons. As usual, we are our catty little selves.

We have developed a running commentary on all the members of the group, including ourselves! "Look at them," you say, nodding subtly to the group we have nicknamed the "over-the-toppers." They are a group preparing for a lengthy marathon, and they are taking the trek to get into shape. They are always, always ahead of the pack. They have no time to experience the beauty of nature. They are on a mission. They are looking for the next challenge to take, even during breaks. "Look at them. They are like race horses stomping at the starting gate. Will they ever slow down?" we chuckle, secretly a little jealous of the elite status they created for themselves.

As we survey the rest of the group, we find ourselves mercilessly continuing: "And, then there's Big Arlette. All she does is look around to see whose pack she can carry and...," we finish each other's sentence, "complains about it at every break when the poor soul who gave her the pack is not within hearing distance."

Not being able to withhold our last impulse, we sneak in, "What's weird is that she's not that big, actually; it's just that her energy is so heavy…." We always move away from Big A.; we can't stand her whining. We continue, "Oh, look at the 'chirpies,'" as we notice the young women who never stop preening around the guide. "You have to admit, he *is* good-looking," one or the other of us says, to remind ourselves we are not totally immune. Just about the time we finish our same old cycle of observations, the guide pipes up. "Ready? Steady, those of you at the head of the path," he says in a tone of authority.

"Always the guide," we laugh, as we slowly get up.

"Aren't we all, always the same?" you say.

"Seems so," I reply, walking to the head of the path, toward clouds of dust left in the wake of the "over-the-toppers," who by now are long gone down the trail.

Cattiness aside, and looking at the "chirpies" who seem to be having a blast, I start to wonder what motivates the limiting behaviors and seeming insecurities we see in each group. I share my curiosity with you. "What's that about?" we start to muse.

To be continued…

IN OUR FANTASY, each group has its own point of view for living in the world. Each group, including us, has a blind spot. The "over-the-toppers" only perceive their mission to excel. The only beauty they see is "their time" and how it might be improving. The "chirpies" don't know they are interesting without having to charm and flit about, working hard to get the guide's attention. I'm sure there are one or two in the bunch, who are smart and natural beauties in their own right. And then there is Big Arlette, who has no clue how dear, warm, charming, and funny she would be if she just stopped complaining. If only she could see self-sacrifice as an unworthy cause.

And then, last but not least, there is us. Imagine all the great walking tips we could accumulate from the over-the-toppers if we weren't busy making sure we were handling the whole arduous experience "just fine, thank you very much. Nothing needed here!" Then, notice how in a moment of insight, we sheepishly share with each other the realization that if we could just get over the thought of how foolish we might look if we were to ask the 'chirpies" to share their girly-girl secrets, we could actually have more fun.

Until we turn curiosity toward ourselves, we are just like the others in the story, blind to ourselves. We are not in the picture of the moment other than from the position of observer. The authentic "What's that about?" attitude, which prompts healthy inquiry into change, only starts at the very end of Our Story.

To facilitate positive growth, it helps to get curious about yourself and the limitations of your character strategy. Of course, this is difficult when you are in the middle of the transition. This is why it helps to bring your focus of attention to the void, the little rift within. To avoid finding yourself in an emotional crisis, you want to take control and actually engineer, widen an opening in the rift so that you may continue to expand beyond the limiting perspective of your character strategy. In Our Story the opening occurred with the insight at how much fun the girly girls were having, to the point of wanting to join in. The insight came about through a question we turned toward ourselves; a question that took us out of our self-reliant frame of reference and into relationship with others.

Let's see what this might look like from an experiential perspective. The little story/metaphor below is to help you see the paradox you face when you try to move and think outside the box of your character strategy.

A Rose is a Rose is a Rose

IMAGINE IF YOU were to ask a rose to explain what it's like to be a tree. From the point of view of the rose, the tree does not really exist in its own right. The essence of the tree is invisible to the eye of the rose. The rose might describe the tree by saying, "Well, a tree doesn't have roses. A tree doesn't usually have thorns. Compared to me, you don't have to take that much care of a tree. For example, you don't have to prune a tree every winter." You can go on and on. The whole perspective of the rose is to use itself as the foundational frame of reference.

To get to the essence of the tree, you have to expand beyond the perspective of the rose. The way to accomplish the task is to create some doubt, an inner rift in the perception system of the rose. Where there is confusion, there is an opportunity for growth. Imagine if you were to quietly say in response to the rose, "How do you know what a tree is like? You are a rose!" The rose would be perplexed. By creating confusion, you have opened the door for the rose to see more. With compassion, you gently lifted the rose out of her self-centered frame of reference into the possibility of a reality that includes other, different, plant life.

Similarly, when you create through awareness a rift in your psyche between the idea of your character strategy and awareness of your authentic, expansive self, curiosity is born. When curiosity is present, the possibility to repair the rupture within is renewed. Basically, from the point of view of your authentic self, there is more to you than your character strategy, even though from the point of view of your character strategy, the rose, this is not possible. Can you see the difference?

I See You!

IF ALL IS going well in our journey, you might be observing that your template for emotional self-care, when based in your character strategy, is not as altruistic as you might like to believe. Remember the chapter where you identified your motivation for helping others? By now, if you are really honest, you may find yourself secretly admitting, with a devilish grin, that your motivation for putting others first is sometimes stimulated by the desire to avoid conflict or emotional pain. Busted! Breakthrough.

Lavender Notes
The limiting aspect of your character strategy is not inclusive of the essence of others, much less the full essence of who you are.

Messy Paradox

Isn't it interesting that, to get your basic trust and safety needs met, you at times rely on outdated material/information that literally keeps you from the intimacy you want? How messed up is that? Now you know why I was giving myself "the one, two" when I landed in the hospital.

I could see how much I got in my own way. What I thought was being considerate of others was in reality a way to protect myself from getting hurt and feeling disappointed. I was trapped and didn't even know it. To be fully integrated, transformational change needs to emerge from the authentic core, the heart.

Armed with this information, I knew I was the only one who could reconnect with my core self. I was the only one who could champion every part of me: my lost self, my little girl, and my inner woman. In other words, I needed to face myself as I was with my limitations and move beyond. I needed to mature. I needed to grow up all over again. I needed to reconnect with the lost part of me and repair the bond that had been ruptured when I was young.

Once I got beyond the "oh, no, there is more to do" factor, I settled down. I explored new perspectives from which to develop a practice of emotional self-care. I used the issues found in my character strategy as flags—indicating where to look for ways to shift.

Lavender Notes

To look beautiful, you maintain your hair. You get it trimmed every so often. Have you noticed that on the day of your hair appointment, your hair starts looking the way you want it to? Through experience, you know you still have to keep your appointment because if you don't, you know for sure a really bad hair day lurks around the corner! The same is true for personal growth. The best time to create shifts is when things are going well.

THE BEAUTY OF WRITING

20. Write Your Heart Out
Theme: *Self-Awareness*

Let's give you a complete felt experience of expanding your inner rift so that you can move through the gauntlet of the transition as easily as possible.

What you believe has more power than what you dream or wish or hope for. You become what you believe.

—

Oprah Winfrey

PREPARATION
- Take a long, deep breath. Hold it for a moment and then let it out slowly.
- Let go of any worry or thought about working "to get it."
- Realize, instead, you have all the time in the world to learn.
- Imagine opening up and flowing forward with ease.

Write down any further self-observations you might have about the impact of your character strategy in your life. Here is a prompt to help.

Prompt: Who would have known that…?

_____

_____

Beauty Metaphor
For supple skin, apply cold cream on your face before you go to bed. Without any effort on your part, you let the moisturizer seep deep into your skin and work its magic at night while you sleep. Curiosity, like cold cream applied to your face, massages your imagination and opens your heart.

A little lipstick, if you please!

While letting inner shifts take place, be gentle, and patient with yourself. Allow the limited belief that tells you to give up, but also make room for hope and the new belief that you do matter.

Inner Glamour Tips
- Please go outside, or look through a window at nature.
- Notice the variety of plants, trees, weeds, birds, cats, and dogs.
- Notice how each plant, tree, and animal takes up its own space.
- Notice the harmony, the disharmony, and the overarching harmony among all living creatures.
- Gently turn your attention inward, and realize you also have a place of belonging in the world.
- As you marvel at the expansiveness of Mother Nature, let yourself feel how she holds the world, with you in it, in the palm of her hand.
- Can you hear the Mistress of the Universe whisper in your ear? "You matter. You are cherished. You were born to express yourself, beauty and soul."
- Take a moment to savor the message. Notice how you feel in your body before you move on.

Outer Glamour Tips
- Take an extra moment in bed in the morning to notice how soft your skin feels.
- As you get out of bed, be aware of not rushing. Let your movements be deliberate.
- Give yourself the message, "There is time for you!"
- Linger in front of the mirror as you put on your lipstick.
- Pause and realize beautiful women have been doing this for centuries.

A lady is never without lipstick.

—

Maureen Corr
(90 years young)
Maureen was the private secretary to Eleanor Roosevelt for the last few years of Eleanor's life. Maureen wore red lipstick.

10

Come to Your Senses

CONTEMPLATE THE IDEA of space contained within infinite space. There are worlds of space all around you, both inside and outside of you. Amazingly, you can expand space imaginatively and retract space with cognitive thinking. The way you play, move, think, and emotionally relate to the space given to you by your birthright is greatly influenced by your core beliefs. For example, do you take up a lot of space? Do you take up too little space? Are you even aware of yourself as a person with the right to take up space? This topic of space does not stem from a narcissistic, "me first" attitude. Quite the contrary, the idea of being a priority in your own life has to do with taking personal responsibility for your authentic emotions, and giving your feelings breathing room. The idea is to always know you have the choice to be first in your life, to believe with all your heart that you matter. The idea is to realize you have the right to choose whose feelings you want to put first, yours or someone else's, and that you cannot escape the inevitable, which is to take responsibility for your choice.

When we are authentic, when we keep our spaces simple, simply beautiful living takes place.

—

Alexandra Stoddard

The Paradox of Taking Up Space

THERE IS A decision process when you decide whose feelings you want to come first. The process involves learning to discern when your decision to put yourself or someone else first is coming from a place of authentic self-care, or if your choice is reactive, based in your default character strategy. Paradoxically, you cannot take up space and put your needs first if you do not first believe from the depth of your being that you are loved, worth it, or that you belong.

The intent of this chapter is to help you shift into the space of your authentic self, where your needs count. You will continue to experientially find ways to circumvent the guards at the wall. You "know" the talking heads are there, just waiting to deter you. It's their job. Learning to foil the sabotage attempts of the guards, as well as putting their incessant hollering to the side, is not an easy task. The endeavor requires self-compassion and patience.

However, you have one advantage. You are now fortified with the awareness that there is another world outside of your character strategy, a mysterious garden full of love and warmth. Although you may not know exactly how to get there this minute, you have what you need. You have the experience of tuning in to the whispers of your heart. You know how to let go and swim in the deep.

All you have to do is be present for what is to come, the challenge and the difficulty, as you take one more step.

Raw Space *(author's story)*

WHAT I HAVE to tell you is not a pretty picture. I'm not proud of the moment. Yet it is a seminal part of my story of opening up. The mini-journey began on New Year's Eve a few years after I was married. My husband was in the hospital and recovering from a surgery he had a couple of days before. As I drove to the hospital, I felt thankful for the positive outcome. We were back on track. As I sat there in the hospital room and the clock struck twelve, I started to have one of the worst pity parties I'd ever had. As I leaned over to kiss my husband, who was experiencing morphine bliss, I suddenly felt sorry for myself. *This is not the kind of New Year's I was expecting to have,* I said to myself. *Where is the fun in this? We should be kissing under the stars somewhere in Paris.* I couldn't believe what was coming over me! Gone was the gratitude and peace I'd felt moments before. I was in the grips of an upset I could not contain. I felt as if a rogue wave had come along and buried me underwater in a sea of anger and upset from which I could not escape. I felt as if I were living in two worlds at once. Like what you see on a split-screen TV, I felt divided down the middle. On one hand, I felt so much love and happiness being able to be with my husband and share the beginning of the New Year. On the other side was a raging child who could only think of the fun she was missing. Fortunately, I did have a couple of wits about me. I knew I needed to take my bad energy—leftover stress, I'm sure—as far away from my husband as possible. I kissed my husband good night and left. On my way home, another rogue wave hit me harder and faster this time. The fury that came over of me astounded even me. That is when I began to have a serious argument with God. Like a youngster having a full-blown temper tantrum at the knees of her parent, I yelled, "Why me? Why us? When is enough…?" I

There are some things you learn best in calm, and some in storm.
—
Willa Cather

screamed at the top of my lungs after making sure all the car windows were rolled up. I yelled and yelled through tears of rage. Utter silence. *At least I wasn't struck dead* was all I could think. Finally, I calmed down. I was spent. I had nothing left in me but empty space and simple tears of regret streaming down my face.

That's when it happened. All of a sudden, I was filled with the most amazing inner peace I had ever experienced. As if by magic the inner division, which caused me so much angst, was washed away and in its place was a new space, a larger space filled with tranquility.

Later, when I got home, I had a new experience. I had the distinct realization that the days of wine and roses were over. I knew intuitively that the journey my husband and I were on was going to require a lot of fortitude and emotional depth. To stay positive, I reminded myself, *It's just a change.* As I sat there thinking, a rush of pain came out of nowhere and took up residence in my heart. *Are you kidding me...there's more?* I wondered, more surprised than angry. I sat there thinking the pain would go away. No such luck; the mistress of pain was there to pay me a visit, and she wasn't leaving anytime soon. As she kept knocking at the door of my heart, I became aware that I needed to make space for her, like you make room for an unexpected house guest. Unfortunately, all the rooms inside me were full. I could not find a way to integrate her into myself. As the searing pain continued, I began to muse, *Is this what it means to become a woman, to be whole, to accept your truth? Nuts to that,* I thought as I went to the shoe closet in my mind to see what pair of shoes might fit this particular occasion. Nothing! There wasn't a single pair of shoes to serve the purpose of knowing how to soothe myself. It was the middle of the night, New Year's Eve. I couldn't exactly call one of my girlfriends. I was alone in brand new territory and experiencing what I believed to be emotional birthing pains. *Fine,* I said to myself as I slipped on my tried-and-true therapist shoes. *Let's just see what occurs if I stay with what is happening inside of me.* I stayed with the experience of pain, just feeling and observing, not analyzing or indulging it. The only thought I had around the pain was that some type of healing, or maturing process, was taking place inside of me.

I had the presence of mind to know I wasn't going crazy or having a panic attack. I knew I was expanding, growing beyond childhood attachments and limitations.

Like the plants I often heard making hissing noises in the still of the night as they grew new stems, I was having a growth spurt. Intuitively, I knew I had to trust that somehow, just as the split I had felt earlier in the evening had resolved itself, so would this. Exhausted, I finally fell asleep.

When I awoke the next day, I felt different. When and how the space inside opened up to make room for the pain, I'll never know. All I can think of is that I didn't run from the pain. I didn't embrace it either. I just stayed with the physical and emotional experience of feeling it, like you might hold a crying baby who is inconsolable. I trusted what I knew: healing occurs within the space of being seen.

New Lessons

IN THE STORY, you can see I hit the wall. The question is, what would have changed the course of that night if I had been more conscious of the self-reliant strategy within? After all, no one ever said I had to be alone in the hospital room on New Year's Eve. In fact, several friends offered to visit and raise a glass of champagne. I just didn't want to put them out, rob them of a good time.

I also did not think of myself as someone who needed support. My nonchalance sent the wrong message. Ultimately, to respect my wishes, our friends left us alone…which is why I ended up feeling isolated. I felt alone because my reality did not include the idea that I needed the nurturing of our friends and family. Would they have been so excited to come to the hospital on New Year's Eve? Probably not; who would? A hospital visit, when someone has had major surgery the day before, is not a party. Yet actions of support go way beyond good times. The idea is about long-term friendship and love. Through my blind spot, I was not aware. I robbed those I love of the good feeling that comes when you express care for others–in this case, my husband and me.

If I had known then what I know now, I would have looked beyond the idea of "I can handle it all myself." I would have actively looked for support and, in the meantime, saved God from having to hear an earful! Can you see where the false motivation of caring for others before consciously checking with your authentic self comes into play?

Blindsided

IN RETROSPECT, I learned that it is selfish to decide what is best for others. You cheat them out of being in relationship and sharing with you what is in their hearts, all because you do not know how to receive. The pain that came knocking at my door that night was pain my strategy could not keep me from feeling. If I had known about my tendency to emotionally isolate, I would not have so been blindsided. I would have welcomed support. Any growth spurt that would have come as a result of what I was going through with my husband would have been organic. The shift into maturity would have been a little softer, gentler in nature.

When it comes to describing the felt process of stepping into the realm of the feminine, I love to refer to a quote I found in the book *Mother of Pearl* by Melinda Haynes (Washington Square Press, 2000). In the book, recommended by Oprah some years ago, there is a moment when a young girl is standing in an anteroom of the house she shares with her aunty. Hidden from view, the young girl is watching her aunty go about ironing while humming a tune. The love and admiration the young girl has in her heart for her aunty is palpable when she says, "My aunty is not like most of the women in town, who only have two sides. My aunty is a six-sided woman; she's lived." Simple, easy, yet so descriptive of the opening-up process.

When I broke through my inner wall, one of the thoughts that got me through the process of letting go of girlhood dreams and opening up to accept the present is that I was growing another side. The awareness gave me comfort. I knew I was not alone. So many women have traveled the path of becoming. Just because my entryway into the garden of the feminine was fraught with pain does not in any way mean that you have to have the same experience. Some of you may be experiencing moments of extreme happiness and are aware that it is difficult to absorb the abundance that surrounds you. You may actually feel your heart aching with joy and know you need to expand. Whether your moment of truth is triggered by difficulty or happiness, keep in mind that you have a choice about what you want to do; you can either grow another side or not.

True Story

IN PSYCHOTHERAPY, THERE is a moment when, through the help of a wonderful little sensorimotor exercise, I am able to help clients become experientially aware of their limiting beliefs. The experiment entails creating a positive paradox within which the voice of the limiting belief is flushed out, heard, and felt by the person doing the exercise.

THE BEAUTY OF WRITING

21. Write Your Heart Out
Theme: *Identification Resonant Belief*

Let's bring into awareness the voice of your limiting belief, which is sure to surface when you stretch beyond your character strategy, most noticeably when you identify and embrace positive thoughts about yourself.

FYI: You are at the wall. This is a moment when the Talking Head(s) come out. As you get ready to do the exercise, the chatter in your mind might sound something like this: "I can't relate to this exercise. This is ridiculous." If you hear any voice that utters similar words, gently shelve the voice. With compassion, let the part of you, the overly protective, guarded little girl, know you are not abandoning her; you will be back later to hear her concerns.

Let's get to the task of establishing your positive belief.

Once you are Real you can't become unreal again. It lasts for always.

—

Margery Williams

PREPARATION

- Take a long, deep breath. Hold it for a moment and let it out very slowly. Do this a few times.
- Align your spine. Starting with your tail bone, imagine releasing one vertebra at a time until you reach top of your spine.
- When you reach the top of your spine, take one extra little stretch to lift your neck and head up out of your shoulders. Breathe into the space you have created.
- From your place of grace, allow an image of your little girl, at her best, to come into focus.
- Create a heartfelt connection with her. Then very quietly, soul to soul, ask for permission to spend a little time with her. Ask her to help you identify one of the positive beliefs below.

Please read slowly. Pause between each sentence. Imagine hearing the voice of someone you love and who loves you speaking these words to you. Read through the whole list before you circle the sentence that makes your heart wake up and pay attention. The sentence may be one you secretly long to hear.

Each sentence represents a healthy belief. Circle only one.

YOU ARE LOVED. YOU ARE SAFE.

YOU ARE SPECIAL. YOU ARE WORTHY.

YOU ARE STRONG. YOU ARE BEAUTIFUL.

YOU ARE FREE. YOU ARE REAL.

YOU MATTER. YOU BELONG. YOU EXIST.

22. Write Your Heart Out (Journal Writing)
Theme: *Resonant Belief Prompt*

To deepen the awareness, keep going. Stay with the experience you are having. Make sure you are connected with your breath as you continue to open up.

Below write the sentence you circled:

_____

When you write, do not look back. Do not edit. Do not pause to think. Let your heart and hand take over. Write as fast as you can and whatever comes into your mind. Use the prompt below, "When I hear the words..."; write the sentence you circled, then continue.

Prompt: When I hear the words... (Write the sentence you circled and keep writing.)

Write in your journal for three minutes.

22a. Write Your Heart Out (cultivating resonance)
Theme: *Limited Beliefs*

Let's check to see if any limiting beliefs surfaced as a result of hearing something positive and wonderful about you. By the way, this is an experiment so you may not necessarily have a negative or limiting belief pop up. The exercise is to test to see if one does, which in my experience is usually the case.

Not until we are lost do we begin to understand ourselves.
—
Henry David Thoreau

A lot of things you can't repair with tales. Try love instead. Try self-love.
—
Mary Oliver

- Take in a nice long breath.
- Center yourself.
- Please go back and reread what you wrote.
- Underline only the sentences that undermine you. They represent the limited beliefs, thoughts and ideas that are buried just below the surface of your awareness. The messages might sound like something the guards would say. For example, "Not true.... I don't believe it.... That's stupid.... You can't go there; you are not worthy." Whatever the sentence is, underline it.

Record your resonant words below.

_____
_____
_____
_____

Can you see how readily the guards pop up, even when you consciously focus your attention on receiving positive input? Unless you actively choose to continually redirect the focus of your attention toward the positive, a part of you is actually strong enough to thwart the positive experience, and thus keep you stuck in the past, in what is familiar. Then you wonder how, in spite of your best efforts to open up and be present, you are not able to do so.

The key is to learn to stay the path of the positive experience, which requires awareness and strength of heart, in spite of the guards and their limiting messages. Fortunately, there is a way to accomplish the task without having to directly confront the guards. Let's take a look.

True Little Story

I once worked with a therapist, Jim, who liked to say, when talking about challenging the defense mechanism, the guards, "You don't have to storm the castle gates; you don't want to get hurt. Just occupy all the territory around the castle so the castle becomes obsolete."

You are in the flow of experience. You are addressing your inner barrier. Hopefully you felt the emergence of your limiting belief in response to the positive belief you identified and then wrote about. As I mentioned previously, a visit from the guards is to be expected. After all, you are messing with their territory. The key is to set about the task of consciously taking up space in the land that surrounds the castle, until the fortress, the old beliefs along with the guards, become obsolete.

Let's use the concept of the castle story as a frame of reference for the work you are doing.

To gain territory around the castle, let's strengthen your emotional tolerance for receiving positive input. To accomplish the task, you will work with your same belief. This time, however, you will frame the experience from the perspective of the first person; therefore, you will own the belief outright.

The most important time in your life is now.

—

Deepak Chopra

Beauty Metaphor
Once you find a rejuvenation cream you like, keep using it. It works.

23. Write Your Heart Out
Theme: *Ownership Positive Belief*

PREPARATION
- Take in a long breath and get centered. Notice the energy in your body quieting.
- Tune into the senses as you might if you were walking in the dark. Breathe!
- Below you will see a list of sentences similar to the ones before. If you notice, the list below starts with the words *I am* as opposed to *You are*.
- Return to the image of your little girl at her best.

- To stay in a state of mindfulness, please take your time as you read through the sentences.
- Notice the belief that strikes a chord with you and possibly makes your little girl smile or gives her a heart ping.
- Please circle the sentence, the clue that resonates with you the most. Do not worry if the sentence you resonate with currently matches what you circled in the last exercise when the sentence started with "You are."
  1. Just stay present and in sync with where you are in this moment in time.

Circle the sentence that most resonates with you.

I am LOVED. I am SAFE. I am SPECIAL. I am WORTHY.

I am STRONG. I am BEAUTIFUL. I am FREE. I MATTER.

I BELONG. I EXIST.

Write the complete belief you circled (above) in the space below.

_____

You are doing great. You are almost there. Now let's integrate the work you have completed by creating a Positive Belief Script, affirmation, for you to practice.

24. Write Your Heart Out
Theme: *Integration Positive Belief*

Please turn to Write Your Heart Out #21 and record on the line below (after the prompt "Yes") the words you circled.

Yes, YOU _____

Now, let's see if there is a match. Notice if the beliefs you selected from Write Your Heart Out, exercises 23 and 24, are the same. For example, if you circled "You are beautiful" in exercise 21 and then chose "I am beautiful" in exercise 24, then you have a match. Your positive script will look like the following:

Positive Belief Script
\# 23. Prompt: I am beautiful.
\# 24. Response: Yes, you are beautiful.

Didn't find an exact match? No worries! If for some reason the sentences you circled don't match, then do the following: If in the second exercise, you circled "I belong," then your positive belief script would read like this:

Prompt: I am beautiful.
Response: Yes, you are beautiful **and** you belong.

Can you see how the positive belief script is a combination of two beliefs that are merged into one belief?

Customize Your Positive Belief Script
Find the example above that describes your experience and use it to write your complete positive script on the line below.

Prompt: I _____
(Fill in with sentence from #21.)

Response: _____

*and*_____

(Fill in with sentence #21 and #24.)

You have done a lot. You have set up a customized positive script you can use to steer you away from the guards at the gate and into the territory around the castle we spoke about earlier.

Retrain Your Brain

When you are ready, read the complete script out loud once and then let it be. Stay focused on the positive experience you have when you read. If any voices of doubt emerge, gently push them to the side and refocus your attention on the good feelings.

Lavender Notes

Sometimes the good feelings that come with the positive script are as tiny as a grain of sand. Fine, that will do. It is a starting place and we will take it!

A little lipstick, if you please!

From the inside out, you are an authentic beauty.

Inner Glamour Tips

Live the truth. Pause several times today and bring to mind the following images when:

- You knew the dress you were wearing looked fabulous and, from the deepest part of yourself, you knew you had your groove on. That woman still exists in you.
- You looked in the mirror and saw the face of a woman in love. That woman still exists in you.
- You uttered a bawdy joke and felt full of passion. That woman still exists in you.
- You made a mistake and laughed out loud. That woman still exists in you.
- You felt the arms of someone special around your waist and it sparked you. That woman still exists in you.
- Now, go for it! See what comes up when you let the woman within you know she still has it going on!
- Realize the woman within you is still alive and kicking.

Outer Glamour Tips

- Color-block what you are wearing with the shade of your lipstick.
- Experts suggest you pair:
  - √ Hot pink with orange
  - √ Coral with purple or fuchsia
  - √ Red with pink
  - √ Cinnamon with melon
  - √ Orange with blue

When I hear the doorbell ring I fluff up my hair; refresh my cherry red lipstick, go to the door ready to greet the world.

—

Odette
(94 years young)

II

Power Shift

WHEN YOU BELIEVE beauty exists, then, when you look for beauty, you find beauty. If, on the other hand, you don't believe beauty exists, then you won't see beauty, even when it is right in front of you. The same goes with personal beliefs. If you believe you are beautiful and someone gives you a compliment, then you will receive the gift with grace and say, "Thank you." If you don't believe you are beautiful, then you won't fully hear compliments, or you will dismiss them because you don't believe such an accolade is possible, at least not for you.

The task of shifting out of a belief that binds your heart and mutes your soul requires more work than repeating an affirmation over and over again. The repetition, when done mindlessly, is the same as pouring a glass of water on arid ground and expecting absorption to take place. No such luck. If you are a gardener, you know that, to soften hardened, claylike soil, you have to use the drip method of watering. Through experience, you trust with patience that the soil will moisten. You know you will no longer

Beauty is in the eye of the beholder.

—

Margaret Wolfe Hungerford

have to worry about breaking ground. All you have to do is keep on watering and fertilizing the soil so that the plants in the garden receive the nurturing they need to thrive.

The work you are going to do in this chapter is a continuation of the work you have been doing. When you identified the missing words you needed to hear when you were little, you began the process of shifting out of limiting beliefs. You broke through the barrier, the hardened crust that hid from view the beauty and soul of your authentic self.

So that the seeds of your core self, buried long ago, sprout and take hold, let's get to watering—slowly, very, very, slowly!

Mountain View *(author's story)*

IT'S NOT POSSIBLE, I thought, my mind reeling. As far as I was concerned, I had arrived at the pinnacle of awareness. I was twenty-something years old! I had just graduated from USC with a master's degree in counseling. As a student in the field of psychology, I was mandated to get into psychotherapy, which I continued upon graduation. On this particular day, I couldn't wait to get to therapy. I had experienced an insight. I knew my new awareness was a game-changer. I was so proud of myself. Feeling successful, I anticipated being told by my therapist that we could begin the termination process. I imagined how cute I would look in all of the new clothes I would suddenly be able to afford!

Finally, I arrived in the parking lot of my therapist's office. Initially, I was not disappointed by my therapist's response. He validated me and lauded my insight. I felt so proud, seen. From there, the session continued and continued with no discussion about ending therapy. A few minutes before the session was to end, I asked, "So does this mean I can terminate therapy?" He looked at me silently for a while, the way therapists can do, then said with a voice full of compassion, "Yes, today you reached the top of the mountain." I felt proud all over again. "It's just that you need to look around to see that it is first of many mountains in the mountain range you will climb during your lifetime." I was struck speechless. All I could think was, "A mountain range! You've got to be kidding…. Isn't one mountain enough?" I looked at him. He looked back at me and quietly said, "You are not done learning; you still have to go down the mountain. In the end, you will be able to climb up and down mountains with ease."

I can still remember leaving his office, miffed and perplexed. I had never thought of life as a mountain range you learned to

It was the first operatic mountain I climbed and the view from it was astounding, exhilarating, stupefying.

—

Leontyne Price

climb. On that day, I began to see. I learned the goal was not to get to the top of a mountain. The journey was to learn to walk amidst mountains. All I had to do was to say yes, give up my new wardrobe, and show up for what was to come next.

Power Shift

YOU HAVE HAD a taste of what it feels like to hear words that have the power to shift your inner experience and thus make a profound difference in your core sense of self. Now, the key is to sustain the opening up process so that you can fortify the part of you that needs to become stronger, the part that needs to learn to walk mountain ranges!

At this suggestion, if you listen closely, you might feel a stirring in your heart. Perhaps you can hear your younger self saying, "Really? Is it true I can be loved, that I can be special?" You may experience the paradox of experiencing the disbelief in juxtaposition with the desire to believe.

Now comes the point of putting together all of the work you have done in the last few chapters!

True Story

MANY YEARS AGO, I was working with a woman who had gone away for a weekend with her girlfriends. When she returned home her husband greeted her at the airport with their two girls, flowers in hand. She told me how happy they were to see her. With tears of joy in her eyes, she said, "You know, for the first time, I actually heard and felt how happy they were to see—how they missed me. With every part of me, I believed them, and it felt wonderful. The funny thing is I have gone away before and upon my return they have always greeted me at the gate with love in their eyes. I just never really took it in. I guess I wasn't paying attention.

Opening Up To Hearing and Seeing

BY EXPANDING AND thus changing the focus of her attention, Sue was able to see beyond her character strategy, which was to always be productive. The kind words and sweet gestures of her husband brought home to her, through her attentiveness, the realization that she mattered. Her capacity to reframe her limited belief from one where she felt unseen to a new belief where she actively looked to see that she mattered provided her with the felt experience that she was seen, that she existed and was loved. By practicing her positive script, she created for herself a transformational experience, one where she felt she existed in her own right, and not because she was a go-getter.

In other words, when she committed to expanding within, Sue began looking with the intent to see and find nurturing in her relationship with her husband. Oriented toward receiving a new experience, she connected with her husband in a new, more profound way. On another level, by opening up and looking to see that she was loved for who she was and finding it, she repaired some of the hurt of the child she was a long time ago, when she felt unseen.

The experiential shift occurs when you slow down, tune into your heart and allow yourself to receive sweet words and kindnesses and/or other words your child needed to hear. Miraculously, your positive script is a game-changer. The simple act of practicing the power of presence, like Sue did, creates an awareness that energetically has the power to shed light on the idea that there is something more. There is love and freedom, beyond the character strategy.

*Over the mountain
there is a path,
although it may not
be seen from
he valley.*

—

Theodore Roethke

THE BEAUTY OF WRITING

25. Write Your Heart Out (Journal Writing)
Theme: *Integration Positive Belief*

Let's give you the opportunity to expand upon your positive script with the intent to help you orient toward seeing and hearing in a different way. Let's use the kind words found in your Positive Belief Script to help you penetrate your garden wall. For the best results, approach the work with deliberation. To get the best outcome, be patient. And don't be surprised to viscerally experience the hyper-vigilance of the guards at the gate.

Think: using the drip method to soften hardened ground to prepare the soil for planting.

PREPARATION
Please read all the directions before implementing them.
- Center yourself with your breath.
- In the space allotted below, write down your positive belief script (found on page 141).
- Read the words of your Positive Belief Script four separate times. Pause between each reading. The pause gives you time to absorb the positive sensations and shifts in thought triggered by the positive belief prompt.

FYI: In the last chapter you focused on finding limiting beliefs. Here you are focusing on the positive experience even though the limiting beliefs are present. Don't let your negative thoughts deter you. Just be aware of them. Put them to the side and get back to focusing on the positive.

Positive Belief Prompt: Record below.

I am _____

(fill in your positive belief)

Yes, you are _____

(fill in your words)

Read Positive Belief Prompt. Record in your journal positive thoughts, feelings, or physical sensations you had as a result of saying and hearing your positive prompt.

Repeat three more times. As you did above, record your experiences in your journal. Make sure you use the Write Your Heart Out number so you can refer back to the exercise at a later date.

Seeing Is Believing

Similar to the princess's physical sensitivity to finding something as tiny as a pea, you can now use your new awareness, new-found sensitivity, to help you stay with your positive frame of reference. To learn to see with your heart, let's explore through guided imagery the micro-moments and movements associated with the unfolding process that goes with opening up.

Our Story: Imagine...

WE ARE STOPPED at the edge of the meandering river we have been following. In the quiet, you feel the intensity of the heat. You hear the buzzing of the insects as they flit about undisturbed by our presence. We have spent the morning talking about self-renewal and what it means to each one of us. We have become fascinated by Mother Nature who, we decided, is our role model for what it looks and feels like to live with the feminine. "You

live, you die, you open up to each new season," we are fond of saying. The words have meaning. They are code to encourage and motivate us to gracefully emerge into the women we are becoming. Specifically, at this moment we are thinking about what it means to own our beauty, our essence. We have come to believe we have to open up and let in the good about ourselves. We have to start seeing and believing in ourselves in a different kind of way.

As you wander around in your mind wondering what the process of opening up looks like, you find the focus of your attention drawn in the direction of a beautiful butterfly circling close by. Entranced, you slow down and get into relationship with the butterfly that you are sure is here to teach you something.

You go into a meditative state…

Attuned, you gently reach out your hand and, full of desire, wait patiently to receive the butterfly. In a state of awe, you energetically experience oneness with the butterfly. You marvel at the palpable beauty and power found in nature.

You hold the moment, yet unfulfilled, waiting for the butterfly's landing. You are rewarded; the butterfly comes closer and lands. You feel physical contact, a slight sensation, a tickle of connection as the butterfly settles in the palm of your hand.

Awakened through sensation, you become aware of the fragility of the butterfly. You feel nurtured as you honor the life you hold in your hand.

After a moment, the butterfly starts to flutter her wings. She's getting ready to fly and journey beyond. Wings spread in full color, she lifts off with exquisite precision.

After she has flown away, you feel the absence of the butterfly's presence. You realize that, even though the magnificent little creature is no longer physically with you, she is with you in spirit. In fact, you notice that the butterfly has left an indelible imprint upon your awareness, carved out a special place of beauty in your heart.

Wistfully, you begin to let go of the moment, as you hold onto the inner space of timelessness. Slowly, you refocus your attention back to where you are by the river. You let out a yawn. You stretch your arms. You get up slowly, ready to resume your walk.

Consciously, you make the decision to trust that the time will come when, once again, you will have the opportunity to bask in the powerful presence of beauty found in nature. You take in another deep breath and realize how good you feel in your body.

To be continued…

Connect with Your Body

DID YOU NOTICE how, in the meditation to create a positive experience, connection, with the butterfly, you closed off all outside noise and focused solely on manifesting a nourishing bond with the butterfly? With the same quiet intent with which you let the butterfly reshape your inner landscape, you are now going to fortify and train your brain to focus on the positive. You started the process in the last chapter when you spoke your positive belief out loud. Now, you are going to focus on multitasking by building the emotional tolerance required to stay connected with your body while you focus on the positive sensations that take place when you open up to new beliefs. Your endeavor supports the development of new neural pathways in the brain that lead to optimal health. This is a two part exercise.

The first exercise focuses on connecting you with your body so that it becomes an integrated part of your awareness for the second part of the process. The idea is that the more you are attuned with your body, the more you have the opportunity to develop the power of feminine presence. With your handy

*Our
aspirations
are our
possibilities.*
—

Samuel Johnson

technique, you can flag what is going on within and then use the information to stay on the path of the positive experience, which I'm sure you just learned is not that easy to practice.

The second exercise is for you to fortify your capacity to orient toward the positive process of the unfolding going on within you, especially when you trade in old beliefs for new core beliefs that really support your authentic nature. Ultimately, the purpose of your two-part task is to learn how to use your inner wisdom to help you stay on the path of becoming and opening up within, which is what the mysterious power of feminine presence is all about.

Lavender Notes

When you integrate a positive core belief into your body, you shift the belief permanently. The belief becomes embodied, as opposed to being just a passing thought. The activity is the difference between just talking about and repeating a positive affirmation and integrating your new belief into the bones of who you are.

PREPARATION
Attention is solely on building the positive experience. If you come across any limiting beliefs, shelve them and refocus.

EXERCISE I: Connect with your body for the purpose of grounding, holding with strength, your upcoming task.

- Please take a deep breath and tune into your body.
- Make sure both your feet are firmly planted on the ground.
- Lengthen your spine, one vertebra at a time.

- Notice if any part of you is collapsed, like your chest or arms. Scan your body for tightness or rigidity. Through your breath, take a moment to release any tension you may be experiencing.
- Notice the sensations you are experiencing in this moment.
- Bring to mind your script, I am… (fill in the words) Yes, you are… (fill in the words).
- Notice where inside your body you experience a warm glow or little sparkle when you say the positive belief to yourself. Only focus on the positive! FYI: The good feeling could be as tiny as a grain of sand or a ping of energy you feel when you hear the special words.

Lavender Notes

Imagine a space, inside yourself, a beautiful shelter within which you cradle the sparkle of warm feeling. The words of your script, coupled with the sparkle, are the seeds of your unfolding.

EXERCISE II: Building tolerance to sustain the positive

Compare your opening up experience to the sweet moment of unfolding, when the butterfly settled into the palm of your hand. Notice what occurs in your body when you say the words and feel the spark associated with your positive script, I am… and Yes, you are… Let's practice.

- Mini-Meditation (Please hold the message of your script in the forefront of your mind as you experience the process below.)
- With a gentle gaze, continue to experience the space inside your body that holds the sparkle.

- Quietly focus all your attention on feeling the positive energy of the sparkle.
- Stay with the experience. As you breathe in and out, just notice the feeling of sparkle, glow.
- Magnify awareness. Notice if the feeling is expanding, contracting, pulsating, or just being.
- If it is moving… in what direction is it moving? Is it moving up and out or sideways?
- Just stay with the felt experience of movement, or non-movement….
- Take your time as you continue to tune in. Breathe as you explore.
- Notice your posture as you let in the good feeling.
- Notice your breath.
- Take a moment to experience the positive sensations you are having in your body.
- Notice if there is an image that goes with your experience.
- Possibly you can sense the presence of the little girl. Intuitively connect with her.
- Gently, say the words of your script to your little girl by using the part of the prompt that says, "Yes, you are_____."
- Notice how she feels as she hears the words you are saying.
- How is she experiencing hearing the words? Is she happy, indifferent? Can she even hear the words you are saying to her? If there is no response, that's okay.
- When you feel ready, create the intent to let the child you were know you will be caring for her. Let her know she is no longer alone. You are there for her!
- Even if you receive a less than positive response from your little girl, let her know you will always be with her. You will love her for who she is.

- Let yourself have a moment to savor this reunion. Let the experience unfold, and flow with it.
- Notice if she has anything to say to you. Are there any other words she wants to hear?
- Stay with the experience for as long as you would like.
- As you get ready to leave and say good-bye to your little girl, tell her you will return.
- Take a long, deep breath and slowly come back into the present moment.

To get centered, take a look around the room. Know you can use the mini-meditation as a short template to create a mind-body connection with your authentic child any time you want to.

Lavender Notes

Reconnecting with the child you were is not new. However, I never felt the reunion to be as powerful as when you connect the imaginative/cognitive experience with the body, which is something I learned through sensorimotor work.

26. Write Your Heart Out (Journal Writing)
Theme: *Reunion Letter*

To foster a felt experience of healing as well as an inner reunion, let's write a thank you letter to the little girl who protected you. The purpose is to create unity between the two of you so that going forward, the wall that divides both of you is no longer invisible or insurmountable.

PREPARATION
- Take a deep breath and imagine you are breathing in strength and peace.
- As you release the breath, re-establish in your mind's eye the image of your little girl.

Help a girl in your life develop a positive relationship with beauty. You can empower her to reach her full potential.

—

Kathy O'Brien

- Ask her what she might need from you. Does she need a thank you for protecting you? Possibly, she needs to hear I'm sorry....
- Take a moment to meditate on this idea to customize your letter.

Please write from one of the prompts below. Do not edit or look back. Write as fast as you can; that way you circumvent the intellect. If you become stuck, just rewrite the last word you wrote as many times as you need to until you write a new word and are back in the flow. For example, it would look like ...like like like like like ... until (new word). Have some tissues on hand. If you cry, write through your tears. Just keep writing no matter what.

Prompts: I thank you for...
I apologize for...
I appreciate you for...

Dear _____ , *(Write in your name, followed by the chosen prompt.)*

Write in your journal for three minutes.

Goodbye Tears of Opening Up

When you let go, it is very common to mourn all the love and compassion you lost out on. If you recall, at the very beginning of our journey, in the third chapter you had a moment to say good-bye. The experience of feeling sad when you let go and open up is normal. The upset is part of the experience of saying good-bye to all the unfulfilled dreams you have so you can start a new beginning, and experience a new lightness of being.

The truth is, your little girl needs to get out of her nursing, caretaking shoes and go barefoot in the grass. Somewhere inside of her, she knows she can count on you because the two of you are part of each other, and you need each other to become whole. She holds the seeds of her growth and you hold the watering can. She knows that, with you by her side, she will be okay, she'll make it. She can blossom and be free; if not now, soon enough.

Coming Full Circle

Through your reunion you are becoming integrated. To fortify your inner bond, take a moment to experience all of the shifts taking place inside you.

A little lipstick, if you please!

The inner woman is there for your little girl. Because of the inner reunion, you can let your inner child, your little girl, know that she can rest. You are present. Therefore, she no longer needs to protect you in the same old way. Gently let her know that you will take over from here on out.

Pink is the one color that makes everyone look pretty instantly, and it will work with everyone's skin tone.

—

Bobbi Brown

Inner Glamour Tips

Let the woman in you take your little girl by the hand.
Together,

- Take a little walk and see what you see.
- Sit in a café and have a drink or relish a piece of pastry. Savor the experience together.
- Ask your little girl what kind of special day she would like to share with you. Follow through and make the day a reality. Possibly she wants to go to the ballet, or the theater. Or, just dance around the living room. Set your voices free, talk out loud; sing or yell if you want to!
- Whatever the choice, allow yourself to enjoy the reunification experience you are creating.

Outer Glamour Tips:

Give those lips a youthful look. Exfoliate.

- Dab a little sugar on soft, moist bristles of your toothbrush.
- Gently brush the toothbrush over your lips a couple of times to remove old skin.

  I'm sure your little girl will love the taste of sugar and you will love how lush and refreshed your lips look.

12

Empower Loving Connection

WITH YOUR LITTLE girl firmly in tow, you are now in charge and ready to head toward the pool of restorative waters nestled in the core of your feminine essence. In this place of wonder, your center, it is easy to get in touch with the mysterious and healthy aspects of your feminine psyche—the young girl, the mother, and let us not forget the inner woman who is the focus of this journey.

To nurture the relationship you are developing with your inner woman, let's deepen your capacity to identify her voice. The task is not simple, because as I spoke about in the beginning of the book, women have a blind spot, which is an over-identification with the role of caretaker.

To refresh your memory, the purpose of your journey is to help you put yourself first, at the top of your priority list. Without the capacity to differentiate between the needs of your inner woman and those of the emotional caretaker, the task of championing your authentic needs is next to impossible.

Mothering myself has become a way of listening to my deepest needs, and of responding to my inner child.

—

Melinda Burns

Not to worry. As promised, support is available. All you have to do is practice presence by mindfully preparing yourself to receive. Allow yourself to feel held, transported as you move through the upcoming series of guided imageries, which are intended to deepen your familiarity with the various "mothering/woman" voices within. Ultimately, I like to think of the cumulative experience in this chapter as the moment your authentic inner woman comes into view and, through heartfelt recognition, you reconnect with her.

Words of Encouragement

IN THIS CHAPTER you will lean on the creative. The chapter is complete with narratives to trigger your imagination so you can release the unconscious material just below the surface of your awareness. You will notice that the chapter is another way of reframing the experiences you have gained in the last three chapters, which of course includes the voice of the limiting beliefs.

When participating in the exercises that emphasize the voice of the positive experience, orient your awareness toward the sensation of sparkle associated with your new authentic core beliefs.

Your intent will fortify your capacity to receive nurturing.

You can recognize the positive experience by the quiet excitement and sense of attunement you have with yourself and the world around you. When this occurs, you know the Mistress of the Feminine is close by and ready to assist you. Think: The drip method is working. However, with watering, some weeds have had the opportunity to flourish. You will have the chance to attend to them as well as continue to fertilize the soil.

Sparkle and Twirls *(author's story)*

THERE WAS A knock at the front door. Christmas tree ornament in hand, I got down off the stepladder and went to answer the door. On the porch stood my neighbor, Nicole, and her three-year-old daughter, Sophie, who was wearing a pretty little red and green twirl skirt. She had tights to match. They were on their way to a Grinch party in the backlot of Universal Studios. "Sophie wanted to show you her outfit," Nicole said brightly. Sophie, standing next to her mother, looked up with a sparkle in her eyes. "Really?" I said, enthusiastically. Sophie's big, bright smile got brighter as she bobbed her long blond curls up and down to say yes. "Let me see," I said with glee.

Sophie stepped forward, delicately holding both sides of her skirt in her tiny hands. "Wow!" I exclaimed. I loved how she was enjoying how pretty and cute she looked. She wanted to be seen. "You should see her skirt when she twirls," Nicole said. Playing along, I responded, "Oh, Sophie, will you twirl for me?" Sophie hesitated. "Oh, come on, Soph, do it just for me. I want to see your skirt!" Shyly, she started to twirl. We both oohed and aahed as she twirled. Sophie was in her element. She knew she was being seen and admired, and with every compliment she became more confident, taller. As the pièce de resistance, Sophie stuck out her leg. "Look," she said sweetly, showing me the red-and-green-striped Grinch tights and little red slippers to match. "Fabulous!" I said.

Satisfied, Sophie took a step back toward her mother and took her hand. There was nothing left to celebrate; the experience was complete. "Well, we'll be on our way. We have to get to the party," Nicole said in parting. The image of Sophie skipping

If we do our jobs right as mothers our daughters will grow from little girls into young ladies rather than raucous women.

—

Caroline Aaron

down the Christmas-lit walkway, chatting as she held Nicole's hand, is one I will never forget. Mother and daughter were one, separate and happy together, enjoying the delight of what it *meant to be feminine.*

The image of Nicole holding Sophie's hand brings the relationship between the inner woman and the authentic child to mind. The picture represents the quality of connection you want to have with your inner child, which is to be open, supportive, communicative, and attuned.

Loving Voices

Please take a moment to notice how Nicole has a parental/adult voice that is separate from Sophie's childlike voice, which is separate from my observing/participatory voice. To repair the rupture caused by your blind spot, you need to be able to identify the various nuances between the authentic and non-authentic caretaking voices within. You literally want to know how to distinguish one voice from another so you will know which voice to focus on when you are making decisions and opening up to the positive core belief.

THE BEAUTY OF WRITING

Three Guided Narratives

Narrative One:
Through the following creative guided narrative, you will be encouraged to create a rift between your old self, the ever-present caretaker of others, and your new self, the authentic inner woman. During the cumulative process, you will go deep into your psyche.

To begin, you will flush out the voice of your inner woman and come to know her heartfelt needs. Subsequently, you will come face to face with the part of you (the über-mother/caretaker, definitely the weed) that tries to sabotage your growth efforts. Finally, in a third process, a true story, you will be shown what it looks like to let go and let love in.

All you have to do is follow along. Give in to the process of opening up your imagination by playing along. Flow with the experience and let the magic happen; the rest will follow.

Expect to feel a little rip, a ping in your psyche that may occur when you become aware of the difference between the overzealous caretaker and your inner woman. As mentioned above, the work is intended to intrigue your imagination and widen the gap between the two parts of you for the purpose of voice identification.

One is not born, but rather becomes, a woman.

—

Simone de Beauvoir

PREPARATION
- Please center yourself in your body.
- To ensure a mind-body connection, read the meditation below slowly.
- The meditation is quite powerful.

Imagine...

You are sitting on an embankment of the most beautiful river. Legend has it that the river runs between and thus unites the head and the heart. Rumor has it that the Mistress of the Mysterious Feminine is known to appear to those sitting on the shores belonging to the heart, which you are now doing.

As you sit, you feel quiet and content. You have journeyed far to reach these shores. The sun is shining softly, caressing your face.

As you gaze across the river, your mind wanders, slowly drifts backward in time to a certain evening.

You are at the Caretakers' Ball, where all the women from the Mother...Hood are gathered to celebrate you and your lifetime achievement award.

You are in your glory. You have a glass of champagne in one hand and your very prominent service award in the other.

You are flush from all the recognition, the wonderful commendations you received about your unwavering devotion and tireless care of others.

Just as you begin to bask in another round of self-admiration, you hear a soft, otherworldly voice coming from behind you, calling your name. Startled, you turn around and time stands still.

There in front of your eyes is the most beautiful woman. She is gazing at you. Her gentle eyes pierce your soul.

She doesn't move. She stands there looking at you, drinking you in. You feel she can read your thoughts.

You feel she sees something in you.

Her look reminds you of something lost; perhaps you know her.

Then you hear the words, "Come. You are invited to enter Woman...Hood." You feel caught off guard; you thought you were already there!

You hear the woman say softly, yet firmly, "The only requirement is to make Woman...Hood your place of belonging, of preference. Unless you have small children, or you are caring for someone who desperately needs you, you have to let your allegiance to the Mother...Hood take second place in your heart."

She pauses, waiting for you to absorb the information.

She notices your hand unconsciously tightens around your achievement award. Still, she waits quietly until she sees your fingers loosen, become more open and relaxed.

Then, in a crystal clear voice, she whispers, "Otherwise, I will not be able to show you the way forward. You will not go any farther than where you are now and you will miss out on becoming part of the inner circle of the wise woman who sits at the hearth of your heart."

You wonder what she means and how you are supposed to do what she is asking of you. She intuits your thoughts. "Do not worry. For now, to get beyond your blind spot, leave behind your mind-set of service and caretaking ways, such as the need to be perfect, to please and charm or go it alone. Only focus on the call of love coming from your heart and you will find wholeness."

You are stunned. What is she talking about? you wonder, even though secretly you know exactly what she is asking of you.

The mystical woman gracefully pauses a moment before she says, "Take your time. I'll be back. We'll talk and then you can let me know what attitudes and behaviors you decide to let go of."

Without thinking, you nod your head up and down, "Yes." You feel a tug at your heart. Even before she is gone, you miss the beautiful woman. You intuit that she is a part of you.

As you contemplate the message you heard, you see the mystical woman fade away. You wonder if you saw a hint of a smile on her face.

You hear a bird chirp. Suddenly, you become aware of your aloneness. You pause. You begin to reminisce. Memories come flooding into the forefront of your mind.

So many times you put yourself second and put the needs of others before your own, even when you didn't have to. You realize how much the impulse to over-nurture others has affected your life, overpowered, and, yes, overshadowed, you, the woman you dreamt you would be.

Slowly, you realize how much of yourself you have given up for love, to fit in, and to keep the peace.

"No wonder I don't feel like myself. No wonder I feel burnt out, dried up. When on earth did I lose my sparkle?" you say to no one in particular.

With the possibility of renewal crackling like electricity in the air, you set your mind to the task of deciding what you are going to let go of.

Full of hope, you feel inspired to write a good-bye letter to the head of the Mother...Hood to relinquish your membership status in the club.

As you process your insights, you feel tingly sensations running through your body. You let out a breath of relief as you realize you are not forbidden to visit the Mother...Hood. You were only told Woman...Hood had to be your garden of preference.

You let out a long sigh. All I have to do is get my priorities straight, you murmur to yourself with awe. With relief in your heart and the sun shining on your face, you set about writing the letter.

27. **Write Your Heart Out:** (Journal Writing)
Theme: *Authentic Assertive Self-Expression*

Be uncensored. Please write fast. You will have time to think later.

Prompt: Dear Ladies of the Mother…Hood,
I regret to inform you that I have had a shift in priorities. I can no longer uphold the credo of the Mother…Hood, which is to put others first before myself. For health reasons I have to let go of …

Write in your journal for three minutes.

You now have the voice of the authentic woman.

27a. **Write Your Heart Out** (cultivating resonance)
Theme: *Voice of Authentic Woman*

Capture the part of your work, your authentic voice, with which you resonate the most.

PREPARATION
- As you have done before, please read your work once slowly.
- Notice which word(s) or sentence resonates the most with your intent to stop putting others before yourself. Or that directly expresses your desire to join Woman…Hood.
- Underline the words or sentence.

Record your resonant sentence on the line below.

_____

_____

Your work is to discover your work and then with all your heart to give yourself to it.

—

Buddha

Narrative Two:

Let's keep going. If you recall, one of the purposes of the chapter is to flush out the various voices you have inside of yourself so that in the future you can readily discern which part of you is talking.

At this point, to accomplish this task, let's continue with the meditation experience, yet from a different perspective, the perspective of the limiting belief. Or you may want to think of it as the voice of the false caretaker, or your ego run amuck!

Tip: To get the most out of the exercise, play. Take on the voice and attitudes of the head of the Mother…Hood and notice what happens in your body.

Imagine:

Building on the story from the last narrative… You are head of the Mother…Hood. You walk with false pride and power. You believe you are the be-all and end-all. No one can touch you. No one dares rival you.

You have just received a letter of resignation from one of your most popular and influential club members. You are shocked.

You never expected her to mature and blossom into someone Woman…Hood would value. You always thought she was rather weak, compliant. Suddenly, you feel hot fire welling up in your belly that you recognize as rage, one of the emotions women of the Mother…Hood are never supposed to show.

To get back in control, you put your smile/mask back in place, quell your toxic fire as best you can, and set about writing a response to your club member, unaware that a part of you, behind the mask, has the intent to cripple the wayward member.

The voice of your toxic fire is not an energy that is easily subdued, and so, with unconscious malevolence and glee in your heart, you write a succinct note you know will do the trick. You create self-doubt in the beautiful woman by turning her authentic vulnerability, her self-perceived weakness, against her!

When you are finished, you take a moment to wonder when she had time to sneak past you and find the entrance to the secret garden, the home of the Woman…Hood.

"Hmm, must fortify the walls around the hearts of our members," is all you can come up with.

You make a note to call the guards.

28. **Write Your Heart Out** (Journal Writing)
    Theme: *Voice of Self-Sabotage*

    Write uncensored as fast as you can. Come from the voice that sabotages and undermines what your authentic inner woman wrote in her letter of resignation. Imagine the voice of a critical mother holding you back, telling you that you are selfish if you put yourself first. Here is your chance to give voice to that voice. Go for it!

    Prompt: Dear _____(Your name here),
    We most definitely cannot accept your resignation from the Mother…Hood because…

    Write in your journal for two minutes.

    (We don't want to empower the voice of self-sabotage. We are using it here for voice identification and comparison.)

    You now have the voice of the inauthentic mother/woman within.

By holding your breath you lose life; by letting go you gain life.

—

Alan Watts

Narrative Three:

Let's now find the voice of the über-mother. The voice with the undermining behaviors and attitudes associated with your blind spot. Your effort will help deepen your awareness of the voice of your character strategy, your false belief—the voice that keeps you stuck, anxious, and closed off from your authentic self.

28a. Write Your Heart Out (cultivating resonance)
Theme: *Voice of Self-Sabotage*

PREPARATION
For great results, use your whole body as a tuning fork.
- Please take in a breath.
- Orient toward the messages that intimidate you into submission, throw you off course.
- Please underline these words and/or messages.
- Record the negative message in the space below.

_____

_____

When you recognize the inauthentic voice that leads you in the wrong direction, away from your authentic core, you can make the choice to move in a different direction and expand out of the familiar tug-of-war pattern. Like a train conductor switches tracks to keep the train running in the right direction, you want to be able to orient toward the voice that inspires and supports you.

To do this, you have to be fully conscious of the voice that tempts you to go off track. Unless you specifically want to work on your undermining belief, you do not have to pay attention to it; you can shelve it.

Lavender Notes

1. When you are opening up, and become stuck, just know that the way to dissolve the barrier is to stay with the physical and mental tug-of-war experience going on inside of you. All that is occurring when this happens, is that the old part of you—let's say, head of the Mother...Hood—is resisting and unable to let go, while another part of you—the inner woman fueled by renewed hope and dreams of possibility—is forging ahead to emotional freedom.

2. The fear coming from the old part of you is a felt physical experience in the body. You can actually feel the strength of the "stuckness," which is literally the inability to open up and let go. To shift the experience, learn to go with what is happening inside of you instead of fighting it.

Let's take a peek at what this looks like. Notice in this next story how subtle the undermining process can be and how important it is to stay with it, while not controlling the tug-of-war process.

True Story

THE WOMAN IN the story is a lawyer. She is describing what it took for her to create an internal shift that came from her heart instead of her head. She was attending a class I was conducting at a local university. Her task was to write daily for thirty days, and notice where her resistance to self-care surfaced. She reported to the group that every day she had her assistant take the workbook down from the shelf (where she kept it in full view) and put it on her desk.

Her Story

She starts with, "It was hard for me to show up today for the workshop. I haven't been able to keep my full commitment to write daily." She continues with, "Every day I looked at that red book and thought, *today is the day I'm going to write*, and every day I was disappointed in myself. For the longest time, I couldn't even touch the book. All I could do was see that darn color red, the color of the book, peeking out from under the stack of reports I had on my desk. For me, red became the color of my resistance, my failure to succeed at the goal I had set for myself, which was to be more open."

She took a breath and continued. "I was frustrated and upset. I wanted to get rid of the book, which I knew I couldn't do because I had to report back to the class. Finally, I came to the conclusion that all I could do was to continue to have my assistant put the book on my desk every day, so at least I could be aware of the commitment I'd made to take care of myself.

"And, true to form, every day, I had to deal with my inability to care for myself. Soon, I realized that, although I had an assistant who made it easy for me, she couldn't do the actual work of caring for my heart, which was symbolized by the gesture of writing. Only I could. Only I could pick up the book and keep my commitment to check in with myself. I was in charge of doing what needed to be done to open up—case closed, no excuses.

"Over time, the presence of the red book, whether it was on the shelf or on my desk, was enough to remind me that I needed to come to terms with how much I wanted to care for myself and wasn't able to reach out and do what needed to be done to accomplish my well-intentioned goal.

"One day, I noticed that I looked at the book with longing as opposed to frustration. Much to my surprise, I found myself reaching for the book. I picked up the book, opened it up, and, much to my amazement, began to write. For me the journey of going inside began by creating an easy access, in-full-view place for my book. Just looking at my book and connecting with the commitment I'd made to myself, along with the sobering heart-felt reality that no matter how hard I tried I wasn't able to be true to myself, created an opening in me that went far beyond my usual frustration and tendency to get rid of, or exit, bothersome situations.

"By staying true to where I found myself, each step of the way, I found a place of emotional longing, a space inside myself I didn't even know existed. The act of connecting to the feeling of longing, which I now realize was a shout-out from my heart to get out of my head and into my feelings, is what catapulted me forward. From there the task of writing, taking care of myself, became easier and easier. Now, I love the color red. For me, it signifies self-compassion and possibility."

Growth Happens When You Stay Attuned

The reason I love this tale is because the woman in the story gives the perfect example of how to transcend self-recrimination in order to create an inner opening, a channel to the beauty and self-compassion within.

To accomplish her goal, the woman in the story did two things. First, she faced the truth, her inability to achieve her desired goal of writing. Secondly, she treated her frustration with gentleness. She kept the state of her disconnect in the forefront of her mind. She connected not only with what she liked, she connected with aspects of herself she did not feel good about. Each step of the way, she stayed connected to the authentic truth.

Aware, she recognized the moment the shift happened. Prepared, she took full advantage of her awakening, connecting with her longing, which triggered the impulse in her body to reach for her book. By staying with the feelings of emotional vulnerability, she nurtured herself and fostered her growth from where she was.

Your Turn

You are going to do the same. You now are going to connect with the strength of the feminine. If you recall, you had a visit from a mystical woman who promised to return. Let's see if and how she might keep her word.

Imagine... *Continuing to build upon the guided narrative.*
You are overwhelmed by the sharp response from the head of the Mother…Hood. You were not expecting such a harsh reply.

Even though you realize you have the tools to nurture yourself, you feel vulnerable, shaken. Yet you feel compelled to join the Woman…Hood. You know, intuit, that it is the right move for you.

As a teardrop rolls down your cheek, you realize you feel weepy in a good sort of way. You allow the release to happen. As you surrender into the warmth of letting go, your heart opens and you find yourself thinking, *I wish I could tune into the power and clarity of the mystical woman. I need her guidance to remind me of my intent to put myself first.* Then, inspired by the twinkling sensation of your inner sparkle, you remember to shelve the messages/letter/negative intent fostered by the head of the Mother…Hood.

You pause. You think, *Maybe, if I believe….* You make the choice to follow the path of trust.

You tune into the sparkle and are reminded of the light of the mystical woman and while doing so create a heartfelt intent to call her forth. Your patience is your prayer.

Then, as quietly as she had previously faded away, you see the beautiful woman gracefully come into view. "You came back" are the only words you can whisper. Through intuitive communion, you hear soft words. "Your trust in me is what brought me back. Your request for support is my invitation to connect with you. You see, you and I are one!"

Somewhere in the back of your mind, you recognize a guilty ping of conscience coming from the direction of the Mother… Hood. Unaware, you flinch. As if she could read your mind, the beautiful woman says, "To be accepted into the Woman…Hood, all you have to do is be willing to trust that you are loved for who you are more than for what you do, which you have done."

Then, in a crystal clear voice, she says with great deliberation, "Once you connected with the shores of your heart, I knew you were ready to let go of false ideas of unworthiness and receive instead the love and nurturing within. Through your willingness to say *yes* to yourself, you came to know that your vulnerability is your strength."

Awed, you say, "There is so much to know," Sensing that you are overwhelmed, the mystical woman says, "This is enough for now. Later I will fill you in on more of the mysteries of the feminine, the codes of the Woman…Hood. For now, here is your membership into our community."

Fully aware, you watch your hand reach out to accept the invitation. Holding the parchment paper in your hand, you feel reassured. You have done what you always wanted to do, which is to reach out and receive. You intuit that this is possibly the meaning of the words "Go Farther."

You let out a sigh as you tell yourself, "All is well." Replenished, you feel confident knowing that through your mind-body connection, you can access the presence of innate wisdom and self-acceptance any time you want to.

You tune back into your life and bring with you the wonder of your experience.

A little lipstick, if you please!

Know you are loved!

Inner Glamour Tips

- When someone gives you a compliment, take it in and say *Thank you*. Acknowledge you are seen and that you matter.
- To feel nurtured, make the long-overdue call to a girlfriend. Let yourself be soothed by the sound of her voice.
- Practice setting inner boundaries by saying *yes* and saying *no*. Notice how luxurious and safe you feel when you protect and take care of the woman within.
- Before you go to sleep, give yourself a big hug and savor the warmth of feeling alive.

I find it a great antidote… lipstick and mirrors and hairspray.

—

Joanna Lumley

Outer Glamour Tips

- Let's put some boundaries around your lips to keep your lips from feathering.
- This is especially helpful if you have tiny wrinkles around your upper lip.
- With a clear lip balm (we love that balm), coat your mouth, going slightly outside the lip line.
- Then, apply lipstick.

13

The Beauty of Presence

THERE IS A time to give and a time to receive. As it is with seasons, you have to know which season is which, to know which activity to pursue. When you get ready to harvest, you mentally prepare to receive the bounties of the land you cultivated. Often, with a sense of triumph and inner appreciation, you survey all the work that has gone before this moment.

In the same celebratory fashion, let's acknowledge all you have accomplished on your inward journey. Let's start by realizing the big breakthrough you brought about as a result of identifying the umbrella perspective of your character strategy. Your new self-awareness has absolutely punctured a hole in your false belief system. The action helped you reach beyond your blind spot, the barrier of limiting beliefs. By leaving the past behind, or at least putting the default role of caretaker into perspective, you stepped into the garden of your authentic feminine with a focus on getting to know the inner woman. Change has occurred. Connections have been made. All is possible.

There is a time for everything. And, a season for every activity under heaven.

—

Ecclesiastes 3:1

A long way from where you started, which was sitting on the edge of the swimming pool thinking about getting wet, you are now immersed in the water and preparing to swim like a fish in the deep end of the pool. You are on the verge of knowing what it means to go with the flow of who you are, realizing you are enough. With opportunity at your fingertips, you are ready to claim the benefits of your inner beauty, your feminine presence. Within the caress of your inner feminine embrace, you are set to practice trust and vulnerability as you let go, relax into your life and receive nurturing.

From your place of centeredness, you are also poised to receive and reintegrate masculine energy, not to dominate but to support. Let's see how.

The Island Has Eyes *(author's story)*

FINALLY, WE WERE on our way. As far as the eye could see was blood-red dirt and bright blue skies. The contrast found in the skirts of Mother Nature was breathtaking. *How could a vision so stark be so beautiful?* I wondered as I thought about how I would tie what I was seeing into the annual retreat I was leading with my colleague, Elizabeth. We were on the island of Lanai, Hawaii. We had left the conference room where we had been writing, for the great outdoors. We were out for adventure. We were looking to experience the feminine instead of talk about it! In our quest to seek out the mysterious, we decided to travel to the spot on the other side of the island where a ship had sunk offshore many years ago.

I was in the lead, driving a bright red, open-aired jeep full of women all laughing and talking up a storm. Elizabeth was driving the second red jeep full of animated women, following right behind on the only two-lane, black-paved road that connected one side of the island to the other. From our perspective, we had the road and the island to ourselves. We were quite the sight with our sunglasses, our hats, and hair blowing in the wind!

About an hour later, we got to our turnoff, a dirt road. With some trepidation, I made the right turn. We all grew quiet as the soft, sweet adventure turned into a bumpy, red-dusty ride. *Not so much fun,* I thought, as I kept my eye on every little ditch and rock that seemed to jump out of nowhere. Silence fell over the group. We were aware that, if we got into trouble, there was no help for miles. Then, the inevitable happened. I went over a mound of dirt road straight into the ditch that seemed to lie in wait. Cautiously, I put the jeep in reverse and the wheels started to spin and spin. You can imagine the rest of the story. Finally, we

Nothing can cure the soul but the senses, just as nothing can cure the senses but the soul.

—

Oscar Wilde

made the call to the rental agency back in town. We told them of our plight. "No problem, we'll have someone there right away," the clerk reassured us. "Right!" we all groaned in unison, thinking our day was ruined.

About five minutes later an old, beat-up convertible with three bulky, twenty-something islanders showed up. "We hear you need help," was all they said. Baffled, I couldn't help but say, "How did you get here so fast?"

"Oh, on the island news travels fast," said the spokesman for the group. Then, with a twinkle in his eye he said, "When you left town, everyone knew there were two red jeeps headed this way." Then he turned to the women in the group and, with an extra dazzle to his smile, added, "We were on the lookout for two red jeeps filled with beautiful women!" Of course, nothing else needed to be said.

On the way back to town, I pondered many aspects of the day. I revisited the idea that even though we thought we were traveling alone, we had company. We were being observed from afar. Unbeknownst to us, eyes full of curiosity and kindness were with us, watching our every move as we playfully enjoyed the visual bounty Mother Nature had provided us with, as we drove from one side of the island to the other.

After the fact, what struck me the most was the quality of disconnect between the islanders who were watching us as we blithely went our merry way, and us, with our total lack of awareness of their presence. They were tuned into us and we were not tuned into them. The whole experience was synchronistic with the theme of the workshop, which dealt with the power of feminine presence, that mysterious presence, beyond our conscious awareness that lives all around us as well as within us.

I like to compare the various after-the-fact perspectives from which to see and be seen found in the story to what it is like to own the feminine experience of the inner woman. Imagine you have this space inside of you, like the island, filled with timeless beauty and inner resources. All you have to do to access the gifts of this amazing part of yourself is to focus on ways of seeing and thinking about yourself as a woman who is different, apart from the caretaker.

Practice Feminine Presence

To FORTIFY THE bond you are developing with your inner woman, always make the conscious decision to walk the path that leads you to your core self. Hold in your mind's eye a space to purposefully embrace the truth that as a woman you not only matter, you have the responsibility to put yourself first. Realize, from a place of strength, that you can love and be loved even when you are vulnerable and in distress.

Masculine Welcome

FEMININE PRESENCE IS not devoid of masculine energy. In fact, masculine energy is very much a part of and in the service of the inner feminine. The two energies do not have to be in a power struggle. The feminine and the masculine can live side by side, integrated into one life force. In the story, we needed muscle to move the car. We got it and received compliments in the process. In return, the young men, the islanders, felt our appreciation and in their own right experienced just how integral their support was to the enjoyment of our journey.

Lavender Notes

The key is: To foster relationship development, it helps to make use of the best of both worlds. You want to benefit from the intuitive, all-inclusive nature of the feminine experience, while being able to function with the clarity of thought associated with the laser-like focus of the goal-oriented masculine energy. In other words, you want to combine both worlds while creating a home base in the world of the feminine. As you can imagine, the process of shifting your home base from one world into that of another is tedious, sometimes confusing, and always messy.

To Find Meaning, Allow Confusion to be Present

IN THE THERAPEUTIC process, when a client is shifting from one paradigm into another, I give them a lot of emotional space. Paradoxically, this is when the client wants direction. It is common to hear comments like, "What do I do with my anxiety when I'm supposed to just be, do nothing?" "How do I deal with feeling lost?" I quietly bring to each person's attention that being lost is a place of knowing, realizing you are confused.

When you make a paradigm shift and venture into the unknown, you can expect to feel lost and anxious. You don't yet know the rules of the road. All that is going on when this occurs is that you are having a minor identity crisis. You are shifting out of a familiar way of being in the world and learning another way to be in the world. So, doesn't it make sense that you might feel a little out of sorts and strange? Just know that if you stay with the experience, like the woman with the red book story in the last chapter, you will start to relax. You will begin to open up.

Lavender Notes

The key is to remain steady and patiently wait for the next step to be revealed to you, which always happens when you mindfully track your upset. Remember, emotional messiness in the middle of transition nurtures the seeds of change you have planted in your heart.

True Story

I WAS ATTENDING a bridal shower. The hostess was giving a tour of her prolific vegetable garden. "This is called a French intensive organic vegetable garden," she said. "As you can see, it is very messy. The vines crawl all over the place and intermingle with each other," she informed us as she pointed to cucumber vines crawling up the stems of huge sunflowers. I noticed that the tomato vines were running amuck amidst the zucchini, yet were full of bright-red fruit.

"Aren't you supposed to remove the flower in between the two stems of the vine to ultimately provide the fruit with more nutrients?" I asked, filled with wonder.

"Nope, not in this garden; everything grows free. Believe me I do not want a garden that I have to work at. I don't have time," she said, smiling as she picked a tomatillo from a vine laced with green beans. "Here, try this. I make green salsa with it."

We all took a bite. "Amazing, delicious," we all marveled.

She then ventured a piece of personal information. "When my mother-in-law comes by, she steps into the garden and begins to critique. She just can't stand the disarray. She likes gardens that are manicured." I looked at the tiny space the vegetable garden took up in the otherwise large, manicured garden. "She doesn't see the value. All she can focus on is the messiness. She doesn't understand how well we sustain ourselves with this little space," she said handing each of us some more vegetables before going back into the house to attend to her other guests.

When a Mess Is Best

LIKE THE HOSTESS's garden, your inner feminine is sensuous and laden with luscious, life-sustaining nutrients. To access the inner resources, trust and give into, as opposed to take control over, the abundance present within you. From the core of your authentic being outward, surrender to the experience of receiving the love your heart unconditionally showers upon you.

THE BEAUTY OF WRITING

29. Write Your Heart Out
Theme: *Wisdom*

I like to think of the story above as a metaphor for what is possible when you tune and reconnect with the inner woman who is ready to reveal to you all of her secrets. All you have to do is continue along the path you are on.

*I accept the
Divine Presence
as now bountifully
expressing peace
and harmony in
my life.*

—

Ernest Holmes

PREPARATION
- Slowly take in a deep breath.
- Turn your gaze inward and find tranquil space within which to receive *good news*.
- Let everything else drop from your focus.
- Allow yourself to become fully aware of the positive connection you are creating.
- Quietly, tune into your heart and listen.

Gently close your eyes and remain still until words reveal themselves to you. Write in the space below the supportive/positive message emanating from that space of tranquility.

_____

_____

_____

Let's follow up and deepen the experience by giving you the chance to integrate the message above into your body. You have done this before. Again you are working on multiple levels to create a mind-body connection with what you are experiencing. Now do the following:

1. As you slowly read the message above, notice how your body responds.
2. Notice if there are any little shifts taking place inside as a result of hearing the message.
3. Notice your breathing.
4. Notice if any other thoughts or images come with your message.
5. Give the experience space. Shelve any non-supportive thoughts. Stay with the positive.
6. Continue to repeat the nourishing words for as long as you like, and notice the shifts, moments of unfolding taking place inside of you.

Now that you are centered in your body, let's continue to deepen your inner experience. From here, you will connect with the guiding light of the mystical presence to evoke a bond with your soul—the inner wisdom within. Ready? You have journeyed far. If I were sitting with you, you would notice the encouraging light in my eyes as I see you open up and go within.

Our Story *(Our Fairy Tale within the Fairy Tale)*

At peace, you are walking in the inner garden adjusting to a new way of seeing. As you look around, you notice all the plant life. As you shift your gaze for a closer look, you notice morning glories lazing about in the sun, fragrant roses proud to show off their thorns, as well as beautiful sycamore trees and mistletoe close by, each contained within their own space. You let out a chuckle as you see cacti with flowers in bloom all scattered about here and there.

Upon close detection, you realize the plants are not used as barriers. Instead, you observe how the character of each plant is strategically used as a beautiful accent to provide fascinating and interesting dimensions to the garden. You muse, "Hmm, so the character of each plant doesn't have to be used as a barrier, it can be used as an accent to make the garden beautiful!" In an aha moment, you make a mental connection when you recognize you don't have change. You just have to modify. "Thank goodness," you say out loud to no one in particular.

From somewhere inside of you, you hear the words, "That's right; you can be yourself."

Curious, you tune in. Tickled, you think, "I'm starting to have a conversation, a relationship connection, with some unknown part of me!"

From afar, the mystical woman within smiles, "That's my girl. Keep going...."

30. **Write Your Heart Out** (Journal Writing)
Theme: *Exploration/Inspiration*

Let's set the inner woman free.

PREPARATION
- Check in with your body and notice what you need to do to become centered.
- Please write uncensored. Keep your focus forward.
- If you get stuck, repeat the last word you wrote or just draw a continuation of circles until a new word emerges.

Prompt: She began to unfold in the most mysterious, unforeseen…

Write in your journal for three minutes.

30a. **Write Your Heart Out** (cultivating resonance)
Theme: *Inspiration/Integration*

While the writing is still fresh, please take a moment to re-read what you wrote. Please find and underline your resonant words.

Record the resonant words from your last writing in the space below.

_____

_____

To love oneself is the beginning of a life-long romance.

—

Oscar Wilde

The more alert and sensitive we are to our own needs, the more loving and generous we can be toward others.

—

Eda LeShan

Before you put the book down for the evening, let's take a moment to review. In the last few chapters:

1. You spent time in the realm of the experiential, where you learned how to live from your heart instead of your head. Ultimately, the goal of your journey is not to deny connection with the cognitive aspect of yourself. After all, you have to think! The purpose of your self-renewal journey is to integrate your thinking process with your feeling process.
2. To accomplish this goal, you started to dismantle the barrier that stands between you and your authentic self, your inner woman.
3. During the process, you shifted from a predominantly masculine point of view, where your feelings are filtered through your thoughts, to an orientation where your feelings are directly connected to and experienced through your heart. In other words, you are *feeling* your feelings instead of *thinking* your feelings.
4. Now, comfortably connected and with everything in the right working order, you are truly ready to reap the benefits of your inward travels.

A little lipstick, if you please!

Focus on being your natural self. Be gentle and patient with your growth process. The inner shifts/changes, like seeds that you water, take time to sprout and blossom.

Inner Glamour Tips (for each character type)
- Morning Glory: Do something frivolous. Avoid adding items on your "to-do list." Put your feet up. Guilt free, read a magazine. Consider the activity productive.
- Fragrant, Thorny Rose: Speak up. Give a straight answer. Don't just go along with the crowd. Say which restaurant or movie you prefer. Consider yourself a woman of value.
- Sycamore Tree Suffocated By Mistletoe: Shake off your shackles. Do what you want. Go out and play. Take time off from being a worrywart. Go to a movie by yourself if you feel like it.
- Cactus: Wake up and party. There are people around! Lose your intensity. Display that flower of yours and notice what happens. If someone offers you an arm to lean on, smile and take it.

Outer Glamour Tips
- Let yourself be pampered! Go to the cosmetic counter at a major department store and get your makeup done for free! Notice what it is like to be fussed over.
- Gift yourself a beautiful cosmetic mirror. Every time you pull it out of your purse, remind yourself that you deserve to be glamorous both on the inside and the outside.

P.S. Are the flowers in the vase still fresh? Are the petals still on the stem?

Most of the women I know need lipstick. It makes them look better and improves their appearance.

—

**Susan Cuddy
(98 years young)**

14

Vanity, Vulnerability and Vitality

WHEN SENSUALITY AND vulnerability are combined together, they create a beautiful essence akin to a signature perfume. Like the allure of a beautiful fragrance, authentic, feminine charisma attracts curiosity, openness, and relationship. You, therefore, need to know how to embody the power and authority granted you. Vastly different from masculine power, which involves dominance, force, and control over others, the power of the feminine invites you to willingly become her partner, so she is free to reveal the many gifts of grace and influence she has to offer.

Love is not
love until love's
vulnerable.

—

Theodore Roethke

Sweet Surrender

IN THIS CHAPTER, you will explore the gifts that come when you emotionally surrender into your heart of hearts. You will work with the receptive, intuitive energy and innate wisdom present in the core of who you are. As I mentioned earlier, your journey of renewal is about building emotional stamina to tolerate the expansion of authentic emotional pleasure. As expected, when you live from your character strategy, the ability to experience heightened pleasure is limited; it has a glass ceiling.

Through stories and examples you will see new ways to shift out of the stunted mind-set of your character strategy to receive the care and nurturing that surrounds you. You will discover the missing experience from childhood that prevented you from fully connecting with the more vulnerable aspect of your nature. Ultimately, before you move into Book Three, you will be able to gauge how far you have come in your journey to shift out of the paradigm of the masculine into the paradigm of the feminine, through a mindfulness questionnaire at the beginning of the next section.

Are you ready to open up some more to discover the sweet side of emotional surrender?

Footloose and Fancy Free *(author's story)*

I LET MYSELF savor the experience of surrendering to the idea that there was no one to care for, except myself! What a treat. My husband was busy, as was the husband of my girlfriend Carole. With a couple of back and forth phone calls between the two of us, we planned a getaway and were now in our rented car cruising through expansive open space toward Enchantment, a resort in Sedona, Arizona. It felt so good to have uninterrupted girlfriend time. As we yakked on, we laughed, joked, and reminisced about our college days, when we had gone to Europe one summer with backpacks. "Those were the days," we kept saying to each other.

As we drove toward the resort that lay nestled on the floor of a large valley between orange-red mountains, we marveled at how many cycles of life we had traveled through together. We were a long way from the funky hostels and inexpensive hotels we had stayed in "way back when." We were splurging. We planned to indulge ourselves with massages, a couple of nice dinners, and a hike to a local vortex known for imparting feminine energy to visitors. We were going to see if we could relax enough to recapture some of the juice we had felt in our much younger days. The motto we repeated with delight to each other spoke volumes: "Just be. Live the moment!"

The next morning, I learned what Carole meant by "Just be" when she said, "I will be a while. I like to take my time getting ready." All dressed and ready to go, I went into the little powder room where Carole was looking at herself in the mirror. She was putting on some makeup. I sat down on a plush stool in front of the mirror. It was obvious Carole didn't want to talk any further. She was absorbed. I became fascinated. "A woman needs to take time to be with herself...to really look in the mirror to see

There is only one journey: going inside yourself.

—

Rainer Maria Rilke

her beauty!" Carole said, putting boundaries around the sacred time she was carving out for herself. I noticed the difference between us. For me, putting on makeup was expedient, not a sensuous experience you indulge in, especially just for yourself! *She's French. She must know what she is talking about,* I thought reminding myself of how so many European women embrace their sensuality with ease. Then, knowing I was going to have to wait, I decided to see for myself what she was talking about. I turned to look into the mirror, straight into my eyes to see what I could see. The one gesture brought me into the garden of my heart.

The next couple of mornings, I followed Carole's lead. I created time and space to bond with my inner woman. On the second day, as I sat there mindfully brushing my hair, I realized how Carole's simple act of staying true to her regimen of self-care helped me get in touch with the capacity to nurture the feminine within myself. As I got used to the idea of looking at and into myself, I noticed how nurturing gestures of self-care for the outer woman reflect the quality of connection I encourage my clients to create with their authentic selves. *Funny how the outside and inside experiences reflect each other,* I mused. Each requires a sense of personal pride and presence of mind strong enough to hold a loving relationship connection with your true self. *There is power in vulnerability!* I thought as I pondered the strength it took to stay present as we accept ourselves for who we are—beauty *and* blemishes!

On the final day of our mini-retreat, as Carole and I drove away from Enchantment, I felt different. I felt restored, and it wasn't because of the massages someone else gave me! I felt renewed because I had expanded. I had opened up a new space within, which allowed me to absorb the sensuous experiences I was partaking in. Open, I experienced the inner feminine to be a place as beautiful and as nurturing as the environment that surrounded me. Oh, how I loved it! As we turned left onto the main highway, heading for the town of Sedona, I realized how in three short days the term "fancy free" had acquired depth and new meaning, a new state of grace.

A Little Vanity, a Lot of Vitality!

WHEN YOU PUT yourself first, you practice genuine self-care that shifts relationship dynamics. Instead of unconsciously igniting power struggles when you get fed up with being ignored, you offer others the opportunity to take a beat, a pause so they can think about how they want to relate to you. Without compromising her beauty routine, Carole assertively not only brought me into relationship with her, she also brought me into relationship with myself. Her not-asking-for-permission stance put me in a position to make some decisions of my own. I could react and think of Carole as selfish, which only means I think my picture is more important than hers. I could pout and play the victim and say, "Well, you could have at least let me know sooner that you would be taking so much time. That way I could have made my own plans," which in my mind was such a waste of energy due to our short vacation schedule. Or, as I did, I could be curious and join her. If I had been in a hurry to get out into fresh morning air before the blazing sun came up, I could have told her I was going to take a walk and would be back in an hour.

Regain the Juice of Youth

THE TRUTH IS, Carole took care of herself and it was up to me to take care of myself! No messiness there other than to sort out what I wanted to do with my space and time. No room for twisted relationship dynamics unless, of course, I wanted to create a scene, which would have said more about me than her. By cultivating mind-body connections within a receptive feminine mind-set, you flow over common relationship bumps with ease. You reduce stress as you remain open with yourself, while staying in relationship with another, which is what healthy relationship is all about.

Let's take a glance at what this looks like from the perspective of our imagined journey.

Our Story: Imagine...

WE ARE ON the crest of a small mountain we have climbed. "I feel as if I can touch the sky," you say from a prone position. Curious about your perspective, I join you. I put my sweater underneath my head and relax into the infinite space above. "Amazing," is all I can say. "Imagine we are just two tiny little specks in the universe," you muse more to yourself than to me. Enjoying the exploration, I add, "Yes, and all the same we do take up space. We have a presence here." "Yeah," we both say in unison, happily triggered by the theme we have been discussing during the length of our journey. We sneak a glance at each other as we silently marvel at how far we have come in understanding ourselves. We even have a new motto: "Play and participate...." The words represent the current theme of "give and receive" that we are exploring. I notice how our new philosophy becomes crystallized with each realization: We have to expand beyond the old self-care concepts if we expect to be the healthy, vibrant women we want to be. Suddenly in synchronicity, we turn to each other and nod toward the group we now lovingly call "our family." "Time to stop talking and start walking," I say, as we both get up to move closer to the group in honor of a decision we had made to consciously open up. "Might as well start practicing wherever we can," you had astutely said on the heels of one of our intense discussions. To bring our goal to fruition, we chose to put aside our judgments, our comfort zone, and focus instead on the beauty of each individual and diversity found in the group.

"Hey, you two," a choir of voices sang out in acknowledgement of our joining the group.

"What little pieces of insight do you two wise owls have for us to chew on today?" We laugh as we settle into the circle. Somehow we like being recognized for our wisdom.

The shift in the group dynamic occurred one day when we were all lazing about during our lunch break on yet another hilltop. We were all in our separate worlds yet linked together by the physical effort we had just endured. Even the "over-the-toppers" were calm. The barriers were down. We were all starting to be a little curious about each other. Much to our surprise, the openness brought forth an unsuspected transformation in each of us. About a half hour before we were to resume the hike, the "chirpies" brought out some mascara and lipstick from their fanny packs for a little refresher, which turned into a mini-makeover session for the two of us.

The session started when the "girly girls" noticed us glancing over at them with interest. We had become fascinated with how much fun they seemed to have just being coquettish. "Just because you're hiking doesn't mean you have to go without. When it comes to beauty, we say, show it off!" Then, as if they heard themselves speak, one of them reiterated, "Of course, we're not going to do eyelashes and such; let's be real." That's when it happened. A couple of the girls said to us, "Here, want to try?" In our new mode of receiving, we looked at each other and replied, "What the heck!" Recognized for being in their element, the "chirpies" relaxed and went to work as they chortled, "Here, a little dab will do it.... There, finished." "Now that wasn't so bad, was it?" said the girl in charge of my makeover.

As I looked into the mirror that had magically appeared from somewhere inside what they called their "survival packs," I couldn't help but say, "I have to admit the new color of lipstick feels fun." I felt a tickling sensation in my stomach. I felt free to laugh, to admire myself, openly. I felt like getting up and dancing. With their contagious enthusiasm, the younger girls gave us permission to play. We accepted, participated, and bonded. Then, the now not-so-authoritarian guide summoned all of us to get ready. The "over-the-toppers," sensing a shift in our energy, yelled out, "We say, let the wise owls lead!" Startled and excited, we both moved to the head of the trail. In a sudden moment of panic, I used my newfound voice: "You'll be there to catch us if we fall, right?" "We've gotcha covered," was all they had to say to reduce my anxiety. I felt a shiver of delight run through my body. *Feels so good to not have to be strong,* I thought as I relished the new experience of receiving support. As we headed down the trail, I heard Arlette say, half joking, "Anyone want to take my pack?" In a spirit of fun and cooperation, one of the over-the-toppers who magically forgot the agenda, shouted out, "Oh, yeah, I will!"

All was well with our little group. We were moving as one. We were playing, learning, and growing together. We were in a flow of giving and receiving, which enhanced who we were as individuals. As we all trailed one behind the other down the path, the sun went behind a cloud. From somewhere behind me, I heard someone say, "Hey, look, Mother Nature is on our side." *Wow, even the over-the-toppers are getting a little woo-woo,* I thought to myself.

To be continued…

Making the Choice to Work It—Feminine Style!

As YOU MAY notice in Our Story, we decided to create a shift in attitude, which incorporated concrete changes in behavior. Our decision allowed us to expand beyond our reactive ways of relating to the world, into another way of being in the world, which is more responsive. By choosing to be open to relationship, we connected to those around us in a way that was fresh, immediate, and responsive to what was going on in the moment. The conscious awareness in attitude made it possible for us to go beyond talking to experiencing the gifts associated with giving and receiving. When the "chirpies/girlies" wanted to play with us, we seized the opportunity. We said yes. They were as delighted to give as we were to receive. Together, we created a complete circle of nurturing, which we all felt in our hearts. Through conscious awareness, we experienced a moment of seeing and being seen.

THE BEAUTY OF WRITING

Let's take a moment to pause and think about how you want to integrate the concept of giving and receiving into your template of emotional self-renewal. What actions, thoughts, or attitudes are you going to explore to help you move through the barrier of your character strategy? What is the missing experience your character strategy over compensates for. For example, as someone who is self-reliant, I have a difficult time leaning. The more self-sufficient I am, the more I do not have to think about needing someone else's support.

31. Write Your Heart Out
Theme: *Self-Assessment/Authentic Needs*

PREPARATION
(*Remember, those with a trauma in your background, go slow!*)
- Take a deep breath and center yourself.
- Allow yourself to be curious. Trust your instincts.

Below is a list of words followed by a questionnaire. Your task is to pair one of the words with one of the questions. Write your answer after the Write Your Heart Out prompt.

Your list of words:
NURTURING
RECOGNITION/ACCEPTANCE
SENSE OF COMPLETION/PEACE
PLAY

Any little bit of experimenting in self-nurturance is very frightening for most of us.

—

Julia Cameron

Questions: *Choose only one word per question.*

1. If you are a woman who secretly believes you are a "good girl" when you are productive and busy, what life experience would you guess you missed out on?
    Write Your Heart Out: _____

2. If you are a woman who secretly believes you are a "good girl" when you are strong and don't need anyone, what life experience would you guess you missed out on?
    Write Your Heart Out: _____

3. If you are a woman who secretly believes you are a "good girl" when you endure and carry the burden of another to avoid their anger, what experience would you guess you missed out on?
    Write Your Heart Out: _____

4. If you are a woman who secretly believes you are a "good girl" when you please others to get what you need, what experience would you guess you missed out on?
    Write Your Heart Out: _____

The Clue in the Missing Experience

Each one of the words above represents a missing experience. The word you wrote down is a specific cue for the missing experience blocked by your character strategy. For example, let's take question number two. If you answered "Nurturing" for question number two, you would be right. Self-reliant women have difficulty receiving nurturing. The inability to see and receive nurturing is their missing experience that, over time, morphed into their blind spot.

Can you see why a self-reliant woman might start to think of ways to lean on others as a way to learn how to let herself be nurtured? Can you see how this helps heal her heart as well as repair the hurt of the original rupture she felt as a child?

Below are the answers for Write Your Heart Out #31
>Number 1: Sense of Completion/Peace (Go-Getter Character Strategy)
>Number 2: Nurturing (Self-Reliant Character Strategy)
>Number 3: Play (Grin and Bear It Character Strategy)
>Number 4: Recognition/Acceptance (Sweet Talker Character Strategy)

True Story

AT THE BEGINNING of a particular Trauma Training weekend, we were given a guided meditation to help us check in with ourselves to see if there was any child part, or parts, that needed resolution.

On this occasion, the little girl who had become the self-appointed guardian of my authentic child showed up. She was the part of me that resonated with the question being asked by the group leader. She answered, clearly, "I need you to take care of me before you take care of the little child. I'm tired, so tired. I too need help, and I'm so little!"

I was startled on two accounts. The first was the realization that there were two parts of me: a very young infant part identified by her protector with the words "before you take care of the little child," and another child part of me, undoubtedly the self-reliant one, who was clearly, for the first time, voicing the need for some nurturing for herself from the adult woman and/or authentic mother in me. I knew this was an important moment, a reunion and a possibility to heal the disconnect that occurred within me when my mother became ill so long ago.

I couldn't believe it (notice the words "not believe," coupled with the act of believing). I was actually experiencing without anxiety from the core outward what it actually felt like to have a need for nurturing. My inner barrier had been penetrated! Miraculously, the part of me muted so long ago was using her authentic voice and learning to trust. She had softened her defensive posture enough to ask for what she needed. She not only shared and voiced her experience of how tired she was (being so little and having to parent herself), but she also clearly stated that she wanted me to take care of her and no one else! There was no pretense or posturing in her request; it was pure, authentic, and straightforward.

Through the experience, I was able to reintegrate the vulnerable little girl who had learned to believe early on it was not okay to have needs for nurturing. By the activity of tuning into and then listening to the request of a younger, not integrated part of myself, along with the capacity and emotional stamina to maintain the experience that was unfolding within me, I was able to move beyond my character strategy.

By staying present with the voice/hurt of my wounded self without judgment, I helped that part of me have a transformational experience that corrected what had happened to her when she was little. Through the strength of our attunement, she was able to experience that it was okay to have needs for nurturing, which literally shifted some of her limiting beliefs. For my part, the key was to stay present without fear or judgment. My responsibility was to give her what she had been missing, which was a nurturing presence that cared about and listened to what she needed.

The process felt like a homecoming. I felt whole with a new, firsthand knowledge that vulnerability is not a power to be feared. Instead, raw vulnerability is the powerful essence upon which intimate relationships are healed and cultivated, including the one you have with yourself.

Lavender Notes

The key is: Once you integrate a disenfranchised part of yourself, the next step is to take responsibility for the needs of that part of you. When you come out from under the role of pseudo caretaker, the most important activity is to welcome and get to know the part of you that was abandoned. The activity will strengthen your emotional capacity to feel whole, integrated. From this vantage point, the woman in you is free to express herself fully without the anxiety of being undermined by a part of you that is still functioning within the scope of limiting beliefs.

Welcome Home Gestures

As I shared with you, I stayed present with the experience of unfolding. During the process, I made a commitment to my younger self: As a woman who has the capacity to nurture/ mother, I would care for her. Like Nicole had taken Sophie's hand, when she was shy and vulnerable, I would help her hold pain, joy, and upset. Most of all, I let her know she was no longer alone. As I quietly reassured the little girl within, I literally felt my body relax. As I stayed with the experience of softening, I felt her become one with me. No longer disconnected, and hidden, she became integrated into the woman I was. I felt myself expand and open up.

True Story

IT TURNED OUT that the next week I sprained my ankle. When my husband showed up at my office with a wheelchair—which, in my self-reliant mind I thought was a little overdone—I said, "Thank you." As I got into the wheelchair, I let myself feel the support he was offering me. True to my word, I kept my promise to the little girl who was tired. I made her a priority and, instead of pretending to be strong, I consciously chose to experience what it felt like to lean. I practiced trust. I opened up, stepped through the wall, the barrier, and let myself be nurtured.

THE BEAUTY OF WRITING

32. Write Your Heart Out: (Journal Writing)
Theme: *Message of Authentic Needs*

Now it's time to hear from any part of you that needs to speak up and express a need.

Stories are medicine… The remedies for repair or reclamation of any lost psychic drive are contained in stories.

—

Clarissa
Pinkola Estés

PREPARATION
*   Take a breath and center yourself.
*   Let an image of your little girl who might have missed out on _____ come to mind.
*   Once you have the image in mind, create the intent to support and listen to that part of you.

The intent is to create freedom of self-expression, from a place of authentic vulnerability.

Prompt: Imagine your little girl saying …

Write in your journal for three minutes.

Now that you have opened up to a missing need, let's focus on some activities that are intended to guide you back into the heart of who you are. For example, if, you are a:

Go-Getter: Learn to experience a sense of completion instead of living in a state of permanent continuum. Know when enough is enough. Find ways to acknowledge yourself for a job well done. Then stop, even if there is more to do. If you have to, make a to-do list and leave it empty.

Sweet Talker: Find actions that fall in the category of truth. Learn to stick to commitments. Speak up. When you are sitting, check to make sure both feet are pointed in the same direction. Learn to experience being seen in full color.

Grin and Bear It: Indulge yourself in moments of play. Realize you are free to make yourself happy. Stop being the scaffold for someone else's house. Become your own shelter, while in relationship. Turn your frustration and resentment into passion!

Self-Reliant: Find ways to let others nurture you, whether you like it or not. Over time, you will learn to like letting yourself be cared for. Learn you are not the only strong one in the household.

Through your experiential process work, you have discovered some buried needs. Now is the moment to orient toward a cognitive frame of awareness so you can create goals that support the new positive frame of reference you are working to build. Below is a list of concrete activities you can use to trigger your imagination so that in the second part of this exercise you can write down goals to support your experience of opening up and developing your feminine presence.

PREPARATION
- Center yourself in your body.
- Use your body as a tuning fork to help you discover the activities that might resonate with you or trigger other ideas that will support the needs expressed in your last writing.

ACTIVITIES
1. Play. Be adventurous. Try on an outfit you may have never thought of trying on before.

Something we were withholding made us weak, until we found it was ourselves.

—

Robert Frost

*Wisdom
is knowing
what to do next;
virtue is
doing it.*

—

David Star Jordan

2. Indulge yourself; find a perfume that suits the woman you are becoming.

3. If you are hosting a dinner party, let a friend who offers bring you what you actually need and not something that sounds convenient for her.

4. If someone asks you what you want for a birthday present, be direct, let them know.

5. If you need a break, take one. Tell your family you are taking time out.

6. If someone is complaining, do not offer to help. It is not your responsibility to rescue.

7. If you receive a flattering invitation and you are overwhelmed in your life, please decline.

8. Give others space for their opinions even if they are different from yours. Notice how interested they become in you when you use silence to create relationship connection.

9. If someone gives you a compliment, say, "Thank you." Let yourself see and be seen.

10. Practice acts of faith. Let go of results. Stay in the space of the "unknown." Allow yourself to be surprised by what emerges.

Let's build on the work you have done. Commit to actions of self-care.

PREPARATION
- Take a nice long soothing breath and realize you have all the time in the world.
- Either select two activities of your own, or draw upon the list above.

33. Write Your Heart Out
(Commit to Action)

Write down two activities.

Two activities I commit to are:

_____

_____

Good for you.

You are consciously creating healthy connections with yourself. You have a frame of reference that encourages and hopefully motivates you to put yourself at the top of your priority list. You are implementing concrete ways to support your path of becoming. Putting the idea of perfection aside, you are successfully changing the relationship you have with yourself. You are reaching within and opening up to a softer and gentler way to live in the world. You are doing this while being in relationship with the masculine aspect of yourself. You are becoming whole.

Consolidating Your Gains
Now, before you leave Book Two, let's take a look through the mindfulness questionnaire below to assess how you are working with the concepts brought forth in this part of your journey.

The intent behind the questions is to provoke insight with the purpose of inspiring you to create meaning for yourself about the journey you are taking.

The real voyage of discovery consists not in seeking new landscapes but in having new eyes.

—

Marcel Proust

PREPARATION
Connect with your breath as you become centered in yourself.

Ask yourself the following questions:
1. When it comes to opening up to a more authentic, loving relationship with yourself, can you see the value in having a more receptive feminine energy? How does this work for you?
2. Are you able to experience the mysterious space within where inspiration works magic?
3. Can you see how important it is to choose the path of openness, even when the path leads to pain, anxiety, or abundant excitement, which puts you in a state of discomfort?
4. Can you see how important it is to build emotional tolerance so you can receive abundance?
5. Can you see how your body is a wonderful tuning fork that can be used to guide and protect you as you venture into the realm of the authentic unknown?
6. Can you see how going with the flow requires a laser-like focus and a thought-out frame of reference from which to mindfully observe the movements necessary to take your next step?
7. Can you see how you use your cognitive abilities even as you are surrendered to the feminine?

Lavender Notes
The feminine embraces the masculine! Once the masculine is surrendered to the flow of the feminine, both united together can be, like Mother Nature, a formidable force to contend with.

A little lipstick, if you please!

Imagine that the Write Your Heart Out exercise above is the perfect prescription for emotional rejuvenation. Imagine yourself implementing the suggestion you wrote down.

Inner Glamour Tips

- Give your heart a little tap with your hand and say to yourself, "Yes, you are amazing."
- This minute connection is very powerful and lets you know through a physical connection with your heart that you are there to care for yourself.
- Repeat often!
- Implement the suggestions you wrote down to support your opening-up process.

I drive with my knees. Otherwise, how can I put on my lipstick?

—

Sharon Stone

Outer Glamour Tips

- When you apply liner to outline your lips, always use a nude color.

BE TRUE
TO
YOURSELF

Book THREE

BE TRUE TO YOURSELF

The true beauty of a woman

is reflected in her soul.

It is the caring that she lovingly

gives the passion that she shows.

The beauty of a woman

grows with passing years.

—Audrey Hepburn—

15

Passing Through the Portals

WE ARE ALL the same. We are all different. What makes the difference between us is how we cross over the threshold of each awakening moment in our life's journey. The manner in which you shift from one moment to the next has to do with the loving relationship you have with your authentic self, as well as the quality of relationship you have with trust, faith, and the mysterious divine.

In this chapter I invite you to continue to "go farther" to discover personal meaning in your life. Take advantage of all the metaphors and guided meditations to find the final piece of your puzzle, the voice of the Mistress of the Universe whispering little gold nuggets of wisdom into your heart. To help your endeavor, you will continue along the path of "seeing and being seen."

Now, let's go find out what messages are waiting for you.

Plant your own garden, decorate your own soul, instead of waiting for someone to bring you flowers.

—

Veronica A. Shoffstall

Travel Advisories

To ENSURE SAFE travels, here are two travel advisories: Remember the motto inscribed on the rock above the waterfall: "Ask and You Shall Receive." As you take your next steps, keep the idea of loving receptivity in mind. Also, as you prepare to dive into the waters of your soul, remember to practice the feminine principles, which are to be curious, playful, intuitive, compassionate, and relational.

Be conscious of the space inside of you and all around you. Be aware of filling the space with your loving "I make a difference" presence. Be conscious and receptive to see and hear the care coming your way. Make sure you shelve the input that feeds your character strategy.

Practice of Presence

A FUN LITTLE formula I came up with to remind you to practice presence is found in the acronym POP. "P" is for pause. You know how to do this. "O" is for observe. "P" is for process. You know how to look, see, and discern with your authentic heart. By using POP, you will be able to mindfully recognize the nuances of what is going on inside of and outside of yourself. Your multi-level awareness will help you make good moment-to-moment decisions when you find yourself at a crossroads as well as help you identify what state of awareness you find yourself in: your character strategy or authentic heart.

My Mother's Eyes *(author's story)*

I COULD VISCERALLY feel my mother watching me as I cut the juicy sweet melon into pieces small enough for her to eat. She was absorbed, gazing at me from her chair in the living room. I could feel her drinking in my presence. I knew she was savoring every last minute of our being together. I felt sadness swell in my heart as I kept cutting the melon, aware of the sacredness of the moment. My mother's health was failing rapidly. Her shortness of breath made it difficult for her to breathe comfortably. She was having trouble walking.

I had always been close to my mother. I knew her. She was leaving. Her life force was waning. As I cut each piece of fragrant fruit, I experienced seeing and being seen in a whole new different way, which brought new meaning to light. The fear of my mother's departure was being replaced by the type of peace and resolution that comes with the desire of wanting someone you love to find relief and comfort. Of course, faith played a large part in the letting-go process. I had wanted to talk about what was happening. With one look my mother let me know her moving on was not something we were going to be discussing. She wanted to embrace life and her children for as long as she could. We were going to *experience* her leaving, not *talk* about it.

I cannot say, however, that the topic of death was avoided. It wasn't. Some of the most memorable moments of our relationship took place in the void, the pause that exists between life and death. The most animated conversations and moments of laughter I had with my mother took place when we talked about her funeral arrangements. Did she want holy cards, flowers? How did she want her hair done and what should she be wearing? Of course, there would be the Holy Rosary! That was my mother, a little bit of vanity and prayer.

Deep in their roots, all flowers keep the light.

—

Theodore Roethke

Then came the moment you always remember, the moment of leaving. It was a Saturday morning. I was saying good-bye to my mother. Her health had failed. She could barely eat. She was having mini-strokes. She was still coherent, just sleeping more. As I was turning to go, she said softly, "I love you, Joanie." There was something in the way she said the words that made me stop in my tracks. My mother was saying a final good-bye to me. I knew it! I turned around and went over to hug her again. She looked straight into my eyes and said the words again. The beauty I saw in my mother's sparkling, translucent blue eyes took my breath away. The light and loving essence that emanated from within her was otherworldly. I felt as if I was catching a glimpse of her soul and seeing straight through to somewhere beyond. My mother was on her way and sharing one last experience with me. She was letting me see through her eyes the Divine she had always believed in.

That was the last time I was to look into my mother's eyes and have her look back at me. Two days later she went into a coma. Mystically, a few moments after she passed on, as I was leaving her hospital room, I heard my mother's voice in my heart as clearly as if she were standing in front of me. She was talking with me, giving some final loving words.

Tying Up Loose Ends

As YOU TUNE into the soul experience, there is only one question left to answer. What to do with the young girl, your guardian at the gate? You can't just leave the overly protective aspect of yourself, the young girl you were, dangling without a reconfigured frame of reference within which to hold and live out her new found belief system.

Our Story: Imagine...

IN THE LAST little while, we reached the final destination of our walking trek. Victorious, we are now retracing our steps, ready to glean every last bit of experience the journey has left to offer us. As we pass by each little rock and clump of trees, we refresh our minds with the memories we made. As we round a corner, we come upon the path amidst "those boulders," which led us to the pond with the waterfall. We pause, both having the same inspiration. "Just one more time," we say to each other. Confident in our hiking ability and capacity to own what is good for us, we approach our guide. "We will catch up with you this evening," was all we had to say as we nodded toward the path. The guide, now mellow, responded, "See you later, then."

Once at the pond, having found our spot, we reminisce. Without much preparation we find ourselves back in the middle of our fairy tale. You start by saying, "We are powerful in our presence. We glow with charisma." Inspired, I jump in: "Yes, and with our newfound strength, we approach the guards with the idea of turning them into friends, giving them a different frame of reference!"

You pipe in. "Now there is a worthy cause!"

I grow introspective. Noticing my quiet, you ask, "What's up?"

Still reflecting, I answer, "You know this is what I do when I work with someone who is opening up!"

Intrigued, you ask, "What do you mean?"

"Well, together my client and I explore the idea of protection. We invite the guard, the sheltering aspect of the client's nature, to befriend and join forces with the authentic, loving woman/ mother within so that protection is based in caring discernment instead of fear-based intimidation, which leads to self-sabotage. I kind of like to think of it as giving the guard a new job with benefits!"

Getting the gist of what I'm saying, you add, "We walk over to the guards with love in our eyes and say, 'We know you are tired. Why don't you rest for a while?'"

With enthusiasm I add soothingly, as if I were talking to the guards, "How about we give you a new purpose? What if you could still have the role of protector and also be at ease?"

In your mind's eye, imagining the guards becoming curious, you play along. You herald the opening and say, "I can see you have the attention of the guards."

Encouraged, and dropping a bit into myself, I continue the discussion with the guards saying, "Yes, we can work as a team. I know we are both tired of fighting each other."

"Now ain't that the truth?" You add, "Sometimes, I can actually feel the tug of war happening in my stomach." We both chuckle and let out a big sigh of relief. It's as if our bodies got in on the act and through the sigh were signaling approval.

We stop, each of us in our own way staying with the opening up and expanding within. Wanting to garner the benefits of the wonderful release and frame the experience, I suggest, "Let's pause to allow the shifts taking place within us to have time to unfold." You nod your head in agreement. After a few moments, I notice a sense of settling. I realize the work is done; integration has occurred. I feel at peace. I turn to you. You look up and complete the fairy tale with the words, "Funny, it's as if I have nothing left to say. I can actually feel the guard part of me saying, 'Okay, then, let there be peace in the garden.'" I can relate. You stop for a moment and with one word sum up the experience. "Wild!

To be continued...

Lavender Notes

You cannot feel safe and experience peace of mind without protection. Like having a front door on your home that you can open and close, the key is to have personal boundaries, as opposed to barriers that lock you in and keep others out. Keep in mind that, to let a garden flourish, you value and protect as well as nurture the space you are cultivating. Let's take a look how protection (the guards) coexists with a practice of presence.

True Story

No SHORTCUTS HERE, I thought as I carefully retraced the steps back along the hardened dirt pathway that led us out of Monet's Water Garden in Giverny, France. I was transported by the breathtaking beauty that surrounded both my sister Annie and me when suddenly out of the corner of my eye I saw something that startled me. An image I could not comprehend registered in my brain. There, in the midst of the lush green undergrowth, almost hidden from view, was a knot of wire encapsulated in a dewdrop of glistening water. *What is this?* I wondered. As I closely inspected it, a wire fence came into view. I discovered that it was a boundary surrounding the garden that contains the lily pond. *Interesting. So it's true!* I mused. *There is only one way in and out of the famous water garden.* The hidden passageway was through a dimly lit underground tunnel that lay at the right-hand corner of the flower garden in front of the classic French farmhouse Claude Monet called home. *Kind of like the path that leads you out of your head into the secret garden of your heart!* I thought as I viewed the beautiful landscape captured in so many Impressionistic paintings.

Freedom in Discipline

JUST AS THERE are rules for love, there are discipline rules when it comes to being vulnerable.

- To be soft, open, and generous of heart, never look to the mysterious in the hopes of abandoning personal responsibility.
- You don't get a pass. When it comes to putting yourself first, learn to use the words *yes* and *no* interchangeably to create permeable, yet safe boundaries.
- Practice the self-care discipline of POP as you take each step into the unknown.
- Having done the work, move forward with an attitude of trust, even if you are being led in a direction you are not crazy about.
- When you doubt, for support use a saying I love that I hear from some of my clients: "More will be revealed."

Lavender Notes

As you already know, there are times when the next footprint you make is fraught with tears. As M. Scott Peck says in his book *A World Waiting to Be Born* (Bantam, 1993), "Sometimes the only consolation you have is to know that the path you are on is your own." I love this quote. I find it so comforting and true.

One of the most amazing aspects of the power of feminine presence is the grace with which you transcend moments of difficulty. Like water that finds its way around boulders with ease, you don't always need a crisis or have to always work on it to open up within. By practicing POP, you can glide with discernment along your path of becoming. When you do this, it is easy to hear the inner whisperings taking place deep in your soul.

Our Story: Imagine...

WE ARE STILL at the pond. We don't want to leave. Behind some distant tree, the sun is about to set. Although the temperature is pleasant, you know from experience the air will soon be cool. Feeling a little pressure, you mentally work your way into taking one last swim, when, suddenly, you notice someone sitting on a boulder nearby. The visitor is still as stone. Slowly, as if she feels the energy of your eyes on her back, she turns to you and smiles. Her crystal-clear eyes, like the glistening turquoise water in the pond, extend a greeting. Transfixed and unable to speak, you smile and just keep staring. The woman breaks the spell. "Are you here to receive grace?" she asks, as if you know what she is talking about. Dumbfounded, you don't say anything. Your eyes say everything. "Oh, I see. You don't know about these sacred waters. Well, legend has it that if you bathe in these waters with a prayer in mind, you will be given a healing, or a message you need to receive." Your eyes go to the carving above the waterfall. "Ask and you shall receive." That's right," she says reading your mind. "In fact, many local women come here to restore themselves."

With that she dives off the rock into the water. Like a mermaid, she swims to the waterfall and disappears into the grotto. You wait, wanting to give the wise woman some private space. You ponder the significance and meaning of asking for and receiving grace. Knowing enough time has passed, you get up, make your way to the boulder, and dive into the pond like the woman before you.

The moment you hit the water, you find yourself swept away by an undercurrent that swiftly carries you to the grotto and plunks you down onto cool stone. Dazed and puzzled, you sit there for a moment. You think you see the wise lady scurry to the back of the grotto, leaving in her wake the message, "Let the waterfall sing to you. She has a message for you. Just ask." You move closer to the veil of water splashing onto rock and water. With a heart open with prayer, you lean forward and put your head under the rivulets of water and fall into a deep trance. You imagine a woman's voice coaxing you. You wonder, *Is this the voice of the mystical woman…?*

To be continued…

Inside myself is a place I live all alone and that's where you renew springs that never dry up.

—

Pearl S. Buck

THE BEAUTY OF WRITING

34. Write Your Heart Out (Journal Writing)
Theme: *Inspiration/Soul Wisdom*

Take out your journal, be prepared, and listen to the song of your soul.

PREPARATION
- Take a nice long breath and then let it out slowly.
- With an open heart and ready to receive, tune into yourself.
- As you listen closely, allow a prayer or message to formulate in your heart.

Write as fast as you can. Do not censor. Finish the prompt.

Prompt: I am the sacred song of your soul. I am here to tell you…

Write in your journal for three minutes.

34a. Write Your Heart Out (cultivating resonance)
  Theme: *Inspiration/Soul Wisdom*

Before selecting a resonant sentence, let's deepen your experience. The purpose is to help you integrate and create a mind-body connection with the writing experience you just completed.

PREPARATION
Strengthen your ability to use your body as a tuning fork.
- Notice if there are any changes or shifts taking place within you as a result of the writing.
- If so, notice each little unfolding take place inside of you. Do this for a few moments.

INTEGRATION PROCESS
- See if there is a word of renewal that goes with your experience. (doesn't have to be so)
- Notice if an image of renewal comes with your experience. (doesn't have to be so)
- Now, let your body stretch and move any way it wants to. (if your body wants to)

Connect with your voice. Find your resonant sentence.
- Slowly read your writing out loud.
- As you read, connect with the sound and tone of your voice.
- Notice the words or sentence that resonate with you the most.
- Please underline your resonant words or sentence.

Record your resonant words or sentence in the space below.

_____

_____

Listening in, we come if we are watchful and reflective to know shade by shade, though never wholly, the person we have been and are becoming.

—

Wendell Johnson

To continue deepening your experience, let's return for a moment to our imagined fantasy.

Our Story: Imagine...

UNDER THE WATERFALL and awakening from the trance you were in, you start to see the world through a different lens. In your heart, you feel a connection with the pool you now believe to be sacred. You have a felt sense of "knowing" the waters you are swimming in. As you contemplate your insight, you hear the words "Yes, like the waters of your soul" coming from somewhere inside. In contrast, coming from the other side of the pond you hear me calling, "Time to get going." Grateful for the shout-out, you ease into the water and swim back across the pool.

A few moments later, refreshed, we start walking back the way we came. As we round the last corner of what we now call "the boulder barrier," you see the wise woman. She is sitting on a boulder, just like before. Her eyes are twinkling as she looks at you. You intuit her talking with you. "Did you hear the song of the waterfall?"

"Yes," you answer.

"Who are you talking with?" I ask.

You respond with a question: "Can't you see her?"

"No," I say.

Being concerned, you drop the subject.

The mystical woman comes to your aid: "She can't see me. I belong to you. I am the song of your soul. Only you can see and hear me."

A little emboldened, you ask without speaking, "How did you get here? I thought you disappeared."

She responds, "Well, there is another way to get to and from the pool without climbing over boulders. You don't always have to work hard to get to a place of opening." Inspired, you make the connection between boulders and defensive strategies. As if reading your mind, the woman continues. "That's right. You don't have to work at it to be open. To access your inner authentic wisdom, just pause, tune in, and wait to hear my whispers. I'm always with you. I live in the garden of your heart. I am part of the divine, the pool of feminine energy you have at the core of your being."

You pause to absorb the information. *Can this be* happening *to me?* you think as you wonder about all of the voices inside of you. Aware and undeterred, the woman continues, "The reason you are drawn to the sacred pond is because the experience of natural beauty resonates with and mirrors what is already inside you!"

You can't describe in words the mysterious truth you feel. You just know you have an urgency to seek. You have to "go farther!"

To be continued...

The nature of human being can only be defined by recounting the history of what we are becoming.

—

Sam Keen

35. Write Your Heart Out: (Journal Writing)
Theme: *Inspiration/Clarification/Go Farther*

No one can tell you how to interpret your authentic experience. The delightful task is yours. The whole purpose of seeking is to find personal meaning through authentic experience. As we revisited the pond, you are now going to revisit what "go farther" means to you.

PREPARATION
- Take a long, deep breath.
- Reflect upon the shifts in thought you experienced since the beginning of your journey.
- Bring your inner woman to mind and muse upon what going farther might mean to her.
- Let the ideas of personal meaning float to the surface of your mind.
- When you feel ready, write from the prompt below. Imagine being held and inspired by the soothing presence of the wise woman from the grotto.

Please write uncensored. More than ever, write as fast as you can to circumvent the intellect. You want the message to come straight from your heart!

Prompt: She woke up inside herself to hear...

Write in your journal for three minutes.

35a. Write Your Heart Out (cultivating resonance)
    Theme: *Clarify/Going Farther*

You have expanded beyond the realm of what is familiar to you, which is the perfect place from which to define what your new self-care practice will look like going forward. So that you create a solid foundation for your self-care practice, you are now going to shift paradigms. For a moment, you will tune into the cognitive/thought aspect of your nature.

    FYI: Notice how you are developing the capacity to be emotionally and mentally adaptive, flexible. You have not only expanded beyond a masculine paradigm to include the feminine, you are now going to experience what it is like to shift back and forth between the two. Keep in mind that you have joined Woman…Hood. Your heart now resides in the authentic feminine.

    Because the following practice consists of working back and forth between experiential and cognitive paradigms, the sequence of exercises will be presented in three parts. The purpose is to have what you see on the page simulate the experience of what it looks like within you.

Lavender Notes
By the way, the capacity to go back and forth, like changing traffic lanes to get to where you are going is called in neuroplasticity in neuroscience parlance. Having neuroplasticity, as you can imagine, is a beauty serum for aging. It keeps your mind young and spry.

*I am
a woman
above
everything
else.*
—
Jacqueline
Kennedy
Onassis

PART ONE: (*Connected with the experiential*)

PREPARATION
- Take a long, soothing breath. Then let it out slowly. Feel your body relax.
- Read your previous writing out loud.
- Find your resonant sentence and underline it.

Record your underlined resonant sentence on the line below.

_____

_____

PART TWO: (*Combination of both the experiential and the cognitive*)

BEFORE WE BEGIN the last sequence of your journey, let's take a moment to appreciate how far you have come in your trek of self-discovery. If you recall, the initial purpose of your journey was to help you reconnect with the feminine experience within. The intent was to revitalize the inner woman and help you forge a heartfelt place of emotional belonging at the hearth of your feminine experience.

On many occasions, you were asked to suspend analytical thought and just flow with the experience of discovery. You were asked to just notice and become aware of your experience without "working it," or working on yourself. By following the path laid out for you in *Lipstick and Soul*, you left your "talking head," or blind spot, behind, and successfully traveled the gauntlet that leads you out of your head and into the authentic realm of your heart.

At this point, my hope is that you realize that emotional vulnerability is not something to be feared. Instead, heartfelt emotional vulnerability is a vital, receptive, and often mysterious aspect of feminine presence, an energetic inner resource that mystically invites love in.

Now, as we near the end of our journey, it is time to reintegrate the masculine paradigm back into the overall picture of who you are. After all, the intent in introducing you to the resources of the feminine was never to get rid of the cognitive, mental aspect yourself, just to expand beyond it. Therefore, in the last sequence of your journey you will be asked to integrate both the wisdom of the experiential, receptive feminine with the more cognitive, analytical knowledge associated with the masculine aspect of who you are. I like to think of the integration of the masculine and the feminine aspects of your nature as mutually interdependent resources. When combined, the two inner resources provide you with the capacity to experientially intuit what feels right for you. Then without fear or the influences of limiting beliefs, you will have the mental clarity to carry out the tasks required to optimize your life.

Now as a member of the Woman…Hood, with the masculine paradigm cradled in the foundation of the inner feminine, you have access to the best of both worlds while living from a gentler perspective.

36. Write Your Heart Out
Theme: *Cognitive Goals/Inner Woman*

Contrary to writing from a stream of conscious awareness, create a focus to be purposeful and discerning. You want the messages to be clear and easy to remember. Take the underlined resonant sentence above and translate it into a practical goal. Make sure, however, that you do not alter the main content of the inspiration you received.

PREPARATION
- Tune into your sharp mind and focus.
- Fill in the prompt below.

Prompt: To nourish my inner woman, I _____

_____

_____

Lavender Notes

You may want to think of the cumulative experience below as weaving together different strands that, when combined, create a single bond, a through-thread that connects you with your deeper authentic self. You are successfully creating healthy mind-body-heart-soul connections, which is one of the main intents of the *Lipstick and Soul* journey.

PART THREE: (*Strictly cognitive*)

Let's now turn to the cognitive so that you can create a more succinct, goal-oriented message for what "go farther" means to you in terms of a practical self-care practice.

37. Write Your Heart Out:

Theme: *Purpose/Meaning for Power of Feminine Presence*

PREPARATION (*Combination experiential and cognitive*)
- Through your breath, tune into your whole self.
- Scan your body to see if your posture is in alignment.
- Tune into and create a bond with your heart. Feel it open up as your mind becomes clearer and clearer.
- Create the intent to trust that all aspects of who you are will contribute to the emerging wisdom you are seeking.

For inspiration, you are invited to turn back and read some of what you have written in the last long writing. To create a concrete mantra and meaning for yourself, you may want to review your cognitive goals. As you are prepared to receive, allow yourself to write down what comes through you. If you would like, you can always perfect it later. For now, just let your wisdom flow.

A renewed sense of purpose for my inner woman is…

_____

_____

For me, the power of feminine presence means…

_____

_____

Wonderful! You are opening up, processing, and integrating all in one sequence of change. You are in the flow of transformation and are doing beautifully!

_____

A little lipstick, if you please!

Inner Glamour Tips

Please enjoy the few suggestions below that represent ways to protect and nurture the garden of your soul.

1. Bring to mind the vase you use for your flowers. Use the vase and flowers as a metaphor for the space of feminine presence within, the garden of your essence.

2. Keep your vase fresh with flowers to remind you of your process of becoming.

3. Become curious about the blossoming process of each flower.

4. Let each flower represent aspects of your inner woman, your sensuality, your passion.

5. Notice how each flower unfolds and, like you, has very distinct characteristics.

6. Bring to mind how slowly and gently the process of unfolding takes place in nature.

7. Imagine the same happening within yourself.

Outer Glamour Tips

1. Nothing is as attractive as fresh breath! To freshen your breath, place a small piece of clove on your tongue and let it sit there.

2. As the clove softens, it releases an explosion of flavor. Be aware of each shift in flavor.

3. Notice how the experience helps you become aware of those sensuous lips of yours.

You can't keep changing men, so settle for changing your lipstick.

—

Heather
Locklear

16

Lipstick and Prayers

FINAL GOODBYES DEFINE the journey. Boundaries that signal a beginning and an ending provide a sense of completion around work well done. When you consciously accomplish the sometimes difficult, yet practical task of letting go, you activate the energy of moving on. With the feminine ever present, you ready yourself for the next phase of receiving.

The final moments between ending and beginning anew is the topic of this last chapter. The seemingly empty *space* between letting go and settling into your new space of being is where many shifts and insights have the possibility to come to fruition, if you are attuned. To benefit from the fruits of your labor, you now want to collect the insights that can easily vanish if you do not mindfully integrate them into your conscious awareness.

The moment is sacred because it contains the space where the mysterious and the ordinary meet to create the alchemy of your destiny. You have done your part. You made the choice to work through your blind spot and thus softened, cracked open,

Learn to get in touch with the silence within yourself and know that everything in this life has a purpose.

—

Elisabeth Kübler-Ross

*I believe
the lasting
revolution
comes from
deep changes in
ourselves which
influence our
collective lives.*

—

Anaïs Nin

and possibly transcended the character strategy that held you hostage. You recaptured the essence of the inner woman as well as created a new template of self-care to nurture her needs.

Overall, you are conscious of the wonderful bond you have with your authentic feminine nature. Your intent to choose the feminine as your place of belonging opened up doors to the mystical. Now, to optimize your capacity to receive, all there is to do is stay present as you have learned to do and allow the seeds of grace you planted in your heart the opportunity to blossom.

The Final Touch *(author's story)*

THE ROOM IN the mortuary was quietly filling up with people who had come to pray the Holy Rosary in honor of my mother. I hadn't been to many such occasions, so I let my aunt take the lead. Now, Kay knew all about rosary etiquette! According to her, you could never have enough rosaries said for you! True to her belief, she had put the small group of mostly women together for yet another round of prayer. The rosary was my aunt's final act of love for my mother.

Along with my family, I sat next to my friend, Christine. Together, we said our Hail Marys and Our Fathers with fervor, a sign of respect for my mother. I intuited that my mother was happy. She loved praying the rosary. In fact, during my childhood we prayed one decade of the rosary, as a family on our knees, every evening. The synchronicity of the moment was not lost on me as I said the final decade of the rosary. "This one's for you, Mom," I said, smiling to myself.

Then the viewing of my mother's open casket commenced. All the guests, along with the rosary brigade, filed by the casket one by one and bid their farewells. Having had a special good-bye moment with my family before the prayer service, I waited until the coast was clear to have one last visit with my mother. Christine in tow, I walked up to the casket. I stood there looking at my mother. She looked so peaceful, dressed in a classic dove-gray pantsuit with her beautiful silver-gray short hair. I paused. Finally, I said to Christine, who was standing at my side, "Something is just not quite right." I paused again, wondering what the difference was. "It's the lipstick. My mother never wore this color lipstick. It does not suit her coloring. She wouldn't like it." Christine nodded.

Then, looking about the room to make sure we were alone, I pulled out the tube of red lipstick I had in my pocket, a keepsake of my mother's. "What if...?" I said as I turned the gold casing of my mother's favorite lipstick. Christine smiled. We were now coconspirators. With a couple of turns, the regal red appeared. With a glance toward the door, just to make sure, I bent down over my mother and slowly began to apply the lipstick. Christine and I could not stop chuckling. "Do you think I'm crazy, irreverent?" I asked my dear friend. "I don't think so!" she confirmed amidst giggles. "Besides, your mother would be happy." "That's right!" I said, laughing, as

I tried to steady my hand. With a little touch of a tissue, all was in place. "There," I said, proud of my work. "Now my mom looks like herself."

Christine and I stood there admiring my mother, my deft handiwork, and our audacity. The gesture of what appeared on the surface to be a cheeky move was a final bonding experience between me, my mother, and my friend. As we turned to leave the room, I felt my mother's spirit laughing with us. No longer confined, she was at peace and joyful—free to play and free to be.

Walking Your Walk

THE ACT OF putting lipstick on my mother's lips while sheltered by my lifelong friend is the moment I truly released my mother to become my own woman. I knew that I had to walk my own path. There was no longer the physical warmth of her loving, understanding embrace to turn to when I got lost or discouraged. I was on my own with the two wonderful resources she had given me: her lipstick tube in one hand and her words "Keep the peace" emblazoned in my heart.

Until that moment, I hadn't realized her words were not to shush my voice, telling me to be quiet. She just wanted me to be mindful. As I walked out of the room at peace and full of an odd joy, I refreshed my lipstick and could imagine hearing her words: "Honey, as you get older, always wear lipstick. It keeps you looking young and pretty." That was my mother; she was still with me, lipstick and soul.

Our Story: Imagine...

We are done trekking. Sitting one last time on the porch where our journey started, we savor our last moments before we return to our families. "We're not gone yet," we tell each other.

Drawn by what has become our habit, our connection to ourselves and each other, we start to reflect. "Funny, we started our journey in springtime and we're ending it in the summer," you muse. "Kind of like the maturation process we've been talking about," I add to your comment.

"I feel so much stronger; don't you? Much more present. I like this idea of owning, I mean giving in to the feminine...now being a woman seems so natural, not so hard-driving. And there is so much power there," I add with emphasis, realizing how much I have changed. I share my insight with you: "Funny, we've lost our edges and gained some sensibility." We then look at each other with that look of ours that says volumes. "Yeah, now we just have to take it out into the world!" we chime in together.

We see the bus coming down the road. We both feel a pinch of sadness. As I let the sadness take up residence in my heart, I hear another quiet voice saying, *Now is the time.* Having learned to listen to myself, I bring out the present I had been hiding behind my back. Surprised you say, "What's this?"

Terrible at good-byes, I try to sound confident in my voice, the leftover, self-reliant stuff I tell myself, as I say, "It's a little something to keep us connected." You tear off the pretty wrapping paper and open the present to find a loosely put-together notebook.

Happy to be sharing with you some of my life's purpose, I tell you, "I noticed you have been writing. So I thought you might like to have a copy of some of the notes I have been compiling for the writing program I've been working on throughout our journey. Basically, the notes are a way of keeping you connected to your heart and helping you keep the feminine alive and dancing."

You don't say much. You had just been wondering how you were going to keep what you had experienced dynamic. The farthest thing from your mind was to be given a gift that would make it easy to nurture your desire. You were certainly not expecting to receive a format within which to contain and organize all your thoughts and insights, much less have them be a vehicle for future growth. "I don't know what to say," you respond.

By the tone in your voice, I can tell you are touched. That is all that matters to me, so I continue, "You can always keep in touch with me."

Just then the bus pulls up. We gather our belongings and take our final steps together. Once ensconced on the bus, we continue our good-byes. "Wouldn't it be fun to meet again?"

I respond to you by saying, "That would be great. We can check in and see how the new relationship we have with ourselves fares with those we love."

"Yeah, now won't that be the test?" you say. "Okay, it's a done deal. We'll meet again and compare notes. I'm sure we'll have a lot to say to each other." We both laugh and then fall silent.

After a moment, I look over at you and see you are napping. By the twitching of your nose and slight smile on your face, I know you are having quite a dream. In fact, you are dreaming that you are strolling toward the natural pool in the garden of your heart. As you approach the soul waters, you hear the chatter and laughter of women of all ages who are bathing there. As you squint to see better, you notice that the women are turned toward you and are greeting you with kindness and compassion in their eyes. You feel a swell of grace rise within as you recognize the young and the old parts that are all a part of you. In their midst sits the wise woman, who has eyes similar to the mystical women who called you to join the Woman…Hood. She has a child resting in her lap. Instinctively, you recognize your wounded little girl. She is resting and at peace. You feel a shiver run through your body. The mystical/divine mother looks at you with sparkling eyes that say, "Welcome home."

To be continued…

The Authentic Relationship

ONE OF THE goals of your self-renewal journey is to own and integrate the various feminine aspects within—the authentic and the wounded, the child and the woman, the mundane as well as the mystical. You have restored and built a wonderful relationship connection between you and your authentic self. With each step you have taken, you reclaimed a piece of your heart. By consciously taking ownership of the inner barrier which separates you from yourself, you liberated yourself to become the woman you are meant to be.

THE BEAUTY OF WRITING

Let's have one farewell cumulative writing to integrate all the explorations.

38. Write Your Heart Out (Journal Writing)
Theme: *Inspiration/Final Cumulative Writing*

PREPARATION
- Please take a deep breath.
- Imagine the mysterious garden within as a metaphor for your authentic self.
- With an open heart, prepare yourself to receive…

Mini-Guided Meditation
Feel a soft refreshing breeze caress your face as you tune into the lush beautiful garden, full of mystical light, and feminine presence. The space is luxurious, full of peace, freedom of movement.

Woman must be the pioneer in this turning inward for strength. In a sense she has always been the pioneer.

—

Anne Morrow
Lindbergh

When I can look
Life in the eyes,
Grown calm and
very coldly wise,
Life will have
given me the Truth,
And taken in
exchange
—my youth.

—

Sara Teasdale

As you go deeper, you intuit how the home of your heart welcomes all aspects of you, the woman, the child—even parts of you that, still unaware, try to lead you down the wrong path.

They are all accepted and all have a voice.

As you gaze at the pool, you become aware of a woman approaching. Upon observation, you see that the woman is you. The community around the pool nods at each other. Inspired, through the voice of the mystical/divine universal mother, the wise woman, they channel and thus offer you a couple of messages…

Write from the prompt. Do not censor.

Prompt: She woke up inside herself to let love in…

Write in your journal for three minutes.

38a. Write Your Heart Out (cultivating resonance)
   Theme: *Inspiration*

While your writing is still fresh, please read your work out loud. Then, as before, underline your resonant sentence.

Record your resonant words or sentence on the line below.

_____

The Final Touch

Your last writing, like putting the final touch of lipstick on my mother's lips, is the good-bye gesture for our journey together. The good-bye completes and bookends a phase in a cycle of your life's journey, a patch of the road I was fortunate to share with you. As with every journey, however, there are a couple of loose ends to tie up. They are as follows:

About Your Customized Journey

From here you will continue on your own until we meet again. Your task will be to keep your garden path clear and free of "emotional" debris that has a tendency to build up when a path is left unattended.

Beauty Metaphor

To keep yourself looking young, you implement a daily beauty routine. In doing so, you take a few moments each day to connect with your outer woman. With the work you have done, you prepared the way for a customized beauty routine to connect you with your inner woman who, just like your skin, needs to be nourished on a daily basis.

So you have a little heads-up about where to find your ongoing program, let's have one last story.

Our Story: Imagine...

We have had our last hug. You are sitting in the airport. With time on your hands, you decide to leaf through the notebook I gave you. As you open up the book, you glance at a page that has the following written inscription:

Travel well, my dear new friend,

Always remember how beautiful and loved you are...even when you are having a bad hair day! No matter where you find yourself, always know how much I cherished our journey together and look forward to spending time with you again. In the meantime, here is a small sample of what you can do with the writings you have done to create an ongoing practice of presence.

P.S. The instructions are similar to ones I give to the women who attend my workshops. Remember always: Be Bold. Be Beautiful. Be True to Yourself.

Joanie

You continue to leaf through the pages of the book until you come to the Appendix Section and you read "Ongoing Write Your Heart Out Practice." Just then, you hear your plane being called. You put the book down gently. You let out a long, deep breath. You refresh your lipstick and think of the "chirpies" with a smile. You realize how you have shifted. You are no longer the same woman who had left home a few weeks ago. You are becoming the woman you always dreamed yourself to be. As you walk toward the gate, you feel a new lightness in your step. You remember who you are. You are a woman who realizes the value of allowing yourself to matter. You know you are better for it! You know that owning your needs not only lets you be your authentic self, but the loving gesture also frees you up to share that part of you, the best of you, with others.

From afar, the wise woman smiles and decides to reinforce your new awareness. She waits until you are napping to impart her message, which comes when you hear the words, as if for the very first time, "For safety reasons, make sure you always put your oxygen mask on first before you attend to others." The flight attendant is looking at you with what seems like a familiar twinkle in her eye. Mysteriously reassured by the synchronicity of the message, you settle back into your seat. As you lay your head back to rest, you feel a sensation of well-being flow through your body. You let out a long, contented sigh, close your eyes and drift back to sleep, thinking you hear someone close by whispering, "Sweet dreams, my dear. I am proud of you!"

All for now….

A little lipstick, if you please!

Be Bold, Be Beautiful, Be True to Yourself

Inner Glamour Tips

Whatever feelings you may be experiencing, hold them with love and grace. This simple process continues the cultivation of peace and contentment within.

- Bring your cupped hands together, palms up, as if you are receiving a gift. Or you may imagine holding a basket for flowers.
- In your mind's eye, gently place in the cup of your hands or flower basket the feelings you have as a result of any exploration you are doing.
- Practice the Observe part of POP by just *holding* and *observing* your feelings.
- Allow yourself to relax or expand as you realize how you are there for yourself. Always remember to live like you matter!

Clients have reported that the visual idea, along with actually cupping their hands together, is reassuring in that it suggests shelter and a place to put feelings of discomfort.

I only have to do three things to look halfway decent, curl my eyelashes, fill in my eyebrows and put some lipstick on.

—

Courteney Cox

Outer Glamour Tips *(Time to Celebrate)*

- To make sure you do not leave a trace of lipstick on your glass when you celebrate, discretely, without touching the rim of the glass with your mouth, lick the lip of the glass before touching it with your lips.
- Now, isn't that a tip worth having?

Afterword

I HAVE ALREADY mentioned to you that I have a difficult time saying good-bye. A leftover Go-Getter tendency, I'm sure. So, of course I would not feel complete until I shared a couple of final thoughts with you. I did not want to say too much at the beginning of the book because I wanted you to have your own experiential journey. Now you have.

I am often asked why I have dedicated this book to women when so many men would benefit from it. I have already shared with you one of my main reasons: Women have a blind spot when it when it comes to the impact of the role of emotional caretaker on their psyche. The purpose of the book was to help you look inside the myth, open up to your authentic self, and thus move beyond the limiting falsehood, which you are now doing.

Now that you are on the track of authentic self-care, I would like to tell you more about the importance of maintaining and embracing your new practice of self-care, as well as offer you some words of encouragement.

As you know, I am a marriage and family therapist, a relationship expert. As I have shared with you, most women are motivated to open up and change as long as they do not have to be too vulnerable. The problem is, as I have said before, you can't really have a thriving relationship when you hold the underlying belief that the act of taking care of yourself will cause irreparable conflict or end your relationship. You can't have an intimate relationship when you hold back your authentic emotions. Along with you, I too have seen too many women stifle themselves, suffer silently, or become ill, all for the sake of unconsciously

May you experience each day as a sacred gift woven around the heart of wonder.

—

John O'Donohue

maintaining the role of emotional caretaker to keep the peace. This reality is not okay. The truth is, it is never okay to go silent, look the other way, or get sick to save your relationship. You matter too much!

The bottom line is that the unconscious denial of self never works when you are striving for emotional health and well-being. Always take care of yourself, which, after all I have said, may paradoxically mean that at times you choose to put others first because the act feels right to you!

So, as we say good-bye, let me give you a heads-up concerning what to expect when you implement your new way of being with those with whom you are most intimate.

To start, I can say that, overall, your relationship will become enhanced as you become more open and free with yourself. I have seen the relationship-reshaping process take place over and over again and, for the most part, the outcome is positive. I will also say, however, that there are those special situations when a woman finally decides to open her eyes and heart to see that she matters and deserves to exist, and her act of self-love destabilizes the relationship for the worse.

To this point, I can also say I have not really met a woman who ultimately doesn't feel better, regardless of the outcome, when she reconnects with and stays in relationship with her authentic inner woman.

So what exactly can you expect when you implement your self-care practice, and put yourself first?

Let's start with you.

I CAN TELL you that, although you feel enthusiastic, you will also undoubtedly feel some guilt, a little disoriented, somewhat anxious, as well as empowered and free, when you put yourself at the top of your priority list. You know what to do. Write, stay the course, and give the process time to unfold. Keep in mind the idea of coexisting emotions and thoughts. Believe me, it is difficult to change. Yet, the process is so worth it.

Now, here are a couple of tips of what you can expect to happen with your partner. I can say for certain that it won't be a bed of roses, so reduce this expectation.

Keep in mind that your partner likely signed up to be with someone who has the unconscious intent to put him first. Now that you are putting yourself first, he may feel a little abandoned or not too happy. So make sure you give him space to catch up with your new way of relating. Let him have his moods and do not jump to his rescue. He's a man; he can sort it out for himself! He will actually start to find a new part within himself, which is the ultimate compliment to you! I would definitely avoid having too many talks. Just stay emotionally present and loving no matter how difficult the endeavor is. With time, when he realizes you are not abandoning him or the relationship, and that you are only caring for yourself, he will start to adapt, slowly, very slowly.

In the meantime, however, his guards will do their best to snag you. When this acting out occurs, stay strong. Believe in your relationship, sometimes even if you have to do it for both of you. Make sure you let him know you care about him at all times. If he is open to it, I would even suggest you let him read this book, which lets you both discuss how to avoid each other's triggers.

Most important, give yourself and your partner lots of time, months, to become whole. Practice patience and refer to the POP exercise mentioned in your book. Always keep your focus on the progress you are making. To develop a positive belief system, keep your eye on the sparkle at the same time you debunk the voice of the guards by sidelining them.

There is so much more to say on the topic, yet we have to complete the work we are doing and say good-bye. I hope to meet up with you on my website, www.lipstickandsoul.com. Make sure you subscribe to the Newsletter so you can benefit with the little tidbits I will share with you about different segments of your book. My site is a work in progress, which I hope will reflect our ongoing relationship. Please feel free to give me your feedback.

I look forward to hearing from you.

Appendix

Customize Your Ongoing Write Your Heart Out Practice.

Please record below and on the following pages the Cultivating Resonant Sentences from your writing. In the future, you may go through the themes listed below and select any writing that fits the mood you find yourself in. The perk is that you are writing from a place of deep resonance on a topic that you are in the process of addressing. The idea is to go deeper while staying safe and in tune with yourself.

When you complete the writing in your journal, make sure you complete the process by finding, underlining and then recording your new resonant sentence as you have done below. By doing so, you are always ready to write and be current with what is going on inside of you.

I highly recommend writing at least once or twice a week. You may want to set up a special section in your journal for your CRSs.

To set up your future writing prompts, simply go through your book, find your resonant work and record it in the matching space. For your convenience the chapter and page numbers of each Cultivating Resonance Sentence are found below. Make sure in all future work you record the Write Your Heart Out number next to your writing. That way you can track your shifts in conscious awareness over time.

Chapter One
1a. Write Your Heart Out (p10) (Writing Theme: Insight/ Discoveries)
From prompt: She woke up inside herself to... Describe insights gleaned from your writing.

Chapter Three
7a.   Write Your Heart Out (p37) (Theme: Insight/Conflict Resolution)
From prompt: Voice of waterfall encouraging you.

Chapter Four
9a.   Write Your Heart Out (p48) (Theme: Contemplation/Self-Respect)
From prompt: Finding what Self-Respect means to you.

Chapter Five
12a. Write Your Heart Out (p65) (Theme: Insight/Wall)
From prompt: Referencing drawing of wall that represents your character strategy.

13a. Write Your Heart Out (68) (Theme: Wisdom)
From prompt: Wise woman whispering in your ear.

Chapter Six
14a. Write Your Heart Out (p79) (Theme: Self-Awareness/Limiting Beliefs)
From prompt: Messages that sabotage you.

14b. Write Your Heart Out /Mind-Body (p79) (Theme: Physical Discernment)
From prompt: Messages that sabotage you.

Chapter Seven

15a. Write Your Heart Out (p93) (Theme: Insight/Awareness of Voice of False Self)

From prompt: Writing from perspective of plant character strategy.

Chapter Eight

16a. Write Your Heart Out (P106) (Theme: Assessment Strategy)

From prompt: Recording identification of strategy/issue most identified with.

19a. Write Your Heart Out (p112) (Theme: Inspiration)

From prompt: Coming upon a fork in the road, she decided to take the path less traveled. As she did, she knew…

Chapter Ten

22a. Write Your Heart Out (p137) (Theme: Limited Beliefs)

From prompt: Limited belief.

Chapter Twelve

27a. Write Your Heart Out (p169) (Theme: Voice of Authentic Woman)

From prompt: Resignation letter to Mother Hood.

28a. Write Your Heart Out (p172) (Theme: Voice of Self-Sabotage)

From prompt: Response from head of Mother Hood.

Chapter Thirteen

30a. Write Your Heart Out (p189) (Theme: Inspiration/Integration)

From prompt: She began to unfold in the most mysterious, unforeseen…

Chapter Fifteen

34a. Write Your Heart Out (p225) (Journal Writing Theme: Inspiration/Soul Wisdom)

From prompt: I am the sacred song of your soul. I am here to tell you…

35a. Write Your Heart Out (p228) (Theme: Inspiration)

From prompt: She woke up inside herself to let love in…

Bibliography

I LIKE THE idea of holding a book in my hands. I like the sensual connection I feel to the paper; it keeps me connected to the sense of touch. Here are some books I recommend reading, or just looking into. They stimulate the senses. These wonderful books support the renewal work you are doing. Some books are oldies but goodies. They have stood the test of time. Some are frivolous, especially the books on beauty. All are intended to create an atmosphere of sensual discovery to keep your inner woman alive and well.

FOR A LITTLE GLAMOUR

Aucoin, K. (2000) *Face Forward*. New York; Little Brown & Company. Provides you with wonderful images of famous historical women to impart information on how to make the most of your eyes and eyebrows. Love it— such a beautiful and sensuous book to look through.

Barnes, S. (2010) *About Face*. Fair winds Press. Shows you amazing transformation techniques using the beauty secrets of top celebrity makeup artists. The book definitely appeals to the glamorous woman within.

Brown, B. (2008) *Bobbi Brown Makeup Manual*. A wonderful and very complete color guide. Fun look at which nail polish color goes with your skin types. There is also a great resource guide at the back of the book.

FOR MENTAL CLARITY AND PHYSICAL FLEXIBILITY

Amen, D., MD (2010) *Change Your Brain, Change Your Body*. Three Rivers Press. If you are someone who likes a lot of scientific information, this is a book for you. The book, although not an easy read, is full of valuable information based on the latest neuroscience research.

Khalsa, S.K. (2002) *Yoga For Women: Health and Radiant Beauty for Every Stage of Life*. London, New York; DK Publishing. Highly recommended by Dr. Christiane Northrup. What more do I need to say? Beautiful photographs of yoga poses.

For Emotional Support

Abrahms Spring, J. (2006) *After The Affair: Healing The Pain and Rebuilding Trust When A Partner Has Been Unfaithful.* HarperCollins. This is a wonderful guide to get your relationship back on track. What I like about her book is that she asks both partners to get involved in the exploration of what went wrong.

Beattie, M. (1992) *Co-Dependent No More: How To Stop Controlling Others And Start Caring For Yourself.* Hazelden. This is a great book, especially if you are living with someone with an addiction. You will gain insight on your own patterns of control.

Miller, A. (1997) *The Drama of the Gifted Child, Revised Edition.* Basic Books. This is an amazing book to read especially if you were raised by a narcissistic mother. I actually have clients tell me to make sure I let others know about this book! This book is definitely an oldie but goody.

Peck, M.S. (1978) *The Road Less Traveled.* Touchstone. This book is definitely an oldie but goody. I love the first sentence which is, "Life is difficult." I read the book many years ago and I know I could read it again and get a lot out of it.

Ross, E.K., MD (2005) *On Grief and Grieving: Finding Meaning Though the Five Stages of Loss.* New York; Macmillan. If you are coping with loss, I highly recommend anything written by Elisabeth Kübler-Ross. Although she is no longer with us, she will always be remembered for her pioneer work on bringing the topics of death and dying into our living rooms.

For Physical Health

Love, S., MD (2010) *Dr. Susan Love's Breast Book (5th Edition).* A Merlyoyd Lawrence Book. The book, authored by one of the foremost authorities on breast cancer, provides you with all sorts of comprehensive information on what to do if you have the disease, as well as how to stay breast-healthy.

Northrup, C., MD (2006) *Mother-Daughter Wisdom.* St. Martin's Press. You may know of Christiane's book *Women's Bodies* St. Martin's Press. This little book is a gem and perfect for mother-daughter discussions.

Schneider, D., MD (2011) *The Complete Book of Bone Health.* New York; Prometheus Press. The book is full of the latest research on osteoporosis. There is a wonderful foreword by Sally Ride.

The Boston Women's Health Collective (2011) *Our Bodies Ourselves, New Edition.* Touchstone. This wonderful book is well laid out by topics and covers all the basics of women's health. I love the idea of women working together to provide us with the latest information about how to care for our bodies.

Viorst, J. (1998) *Necessary Losses.* New York; Simon & Schuster. I have had so many women tell me how much they love and felt comforted when reading this book.

For Beautiful Skin

Wu, J., MD, (2011) *Feed Your Face.* St. Martin's Press. Very current. Now here is a book which is full of wonderful information as well as fun to read. You will find everything you need to know about caring for your skin and more.

> Please remember your public library!
>
> To keep yourself mentally fit, read a magazine you might not ordinarily pick up. To stimulate your senses, pick up a copy of *National Geographic* magazine. To stimulate your palate, read *Bon Appetit.* Read travel magazines to keep you dreaming and your imaginative alive.
>
> For women with special needs, or who would like to explore further, here is some information I hope will help:

Websites and Phone Numbers for
Referral Information on Organizations

Alcoholics Anonymous (AA) www.alcoholicsanonymous.org (free). Perfect resource if you think you have a drinking problem and feel in need of help. When you attend a meeting for the first time, you will be called a "newcomer." Just know that you can remain anonymous and do not have to raise your hand. If, however, you would like support, I suggest you raise your hand so someone comes over at the break to talk with you. Also, if a man suggests that he give you his phone number, be a little dubious. The tradition is that men do not sponsor women in their recovery effort, although they may be friendly and supportive. Otherwise, feel free to take the number of anyone who offers their number to you. The offer is genuine and may save your life.

Al-Anon (free) www.alanon.org. For anyone close to an alcoholic (sober or not) and needs emotional support to cope with the pain. The meetings, if they are based in health, can be a wonderful source of inspiration.

American Cancer Society www.cancer.org. A wonderful place to begin a generic search to familiarize yourself with the disease.

More on Cancer

Dr. Susan Love Research Foundation www.drsusanloveresearchfoundation.org. The site provides a host of information on latest research, books, and other up-to-date information. The website deserves a Favorite marker if you are battling cancer. If not, the site is definitely worth checking out anyway.

A pertinent website referred to by Dr. Love is www.y.me.org The website and hotline provide direction for clinical questions to ask your doctor. The twenty-four-hour hotline phone number is 800 221-2141 for English, or Spanish 800 986-9505.

Co-Dependents Anonymous or Coda (free) www.codependency.org. Wonderful resource if you feel you are enmeshed in your relationship and are seeking accountability and support to become more independent. Make sure, however, that when you look for a meeting, you look for healthy interactions among the group members. Some meetings have healthier members than others. Sometimes there is a mix. Focus on the members who are healthy and not so concerned about drama. You will notice the difference when you listen to the various members speak.

American Heart Association www.americanheartassociation.org. Always think of being heart-healthy. Get your checkups regularly. With the type of stress you are under today, taking care of your health is of the utmost importance.

National Adoption Information Clearing House www.naic.acf.hhs.gov.

National Domestic Violence Hotline www.ndvh.org. 800 799-7233 or 800 787-3224. Please do not hesitate. You need to have support when you need it! Do not try to be strong and pretend it doesn't matter. When you deny domestic violence, the cycles of abuse can tend to get worse. In the process, you lose your self-esteem.

Rape, Abuse & Incest National Network (RAINN) www.rainn.org. Hotline for survivors of sexual assault 800 656-4673 Please do not wait. Get support immediately; you need it. Talking, at your own pace, will help you begin to heal the trauma you have experienced.

U.S. Department of Justice, Office on Violence Against Women www.ojp.usdog.gov/vawo/ 202 307-6026 or 202 307-2277 Same as all of the above.